The Lived Experience of
Group Spiritual Direction

The Lived Experience of Group Spiritual Direction

Edited by
Rose Mary Dougherty, S.S.N.D.,
with Monica Maxon and Lynne Smith

Foreword by Tilden Edwards

Paulist Press
New York/Mahwah, N.J.

The scripture quotations contained in "Group Spiritual Direction with Clergy" are from the New Revised Standard Version Bible, copyright © 1989 by the Division of Christian Education of the National Council of the Churches of Christ in the U.S.A., and are used by permission. All rights reserved.

Book design by Lynn Else
Cover design by Lynn Else

Library of Congress Cataloging-in-Publication Data

The lived experience of group spiritual direction / edited by Rose Mary Dougherty with Monica Maxon and Lynne Smith.
    p.   cm.
  Includes bibliographical references.
  ISBN 0-8091-4176-0
  1. Spiritual direction. 2. Church group work. I. Dougherty, Rose Mary, 1939- II. Maxon, Monica. III. Smith, Lynne.
BV5053 .L59 2003
253.5'3—dc21

                                                        2003006026

Published by Paulist Press
997 Macarthur Boulevard
Mahwah, New Jersey 07430

www.paulistpress.com

Printed and bound in the
United States of America

Contents

Contents

Contents

*This book is written in deep appreciation
for the long-term participants
in group spiritual direction at Shalem —
for all they have taught us
through their process of faithful listening.*

The Only Light You Can't See
Gigi Ross

On a center plank we kneel
hang on every silence.
Wait for what can never be.
What we lost when we thought
we knew where we were going.

Eyes closed, reading this.
Not the flame we expected.
Let me be your silent beginning.

The only light, candle-quiver.
Wax drops on wood.

Foreword

Long ago, Saint Augustine realized that our hearts are restless until they rest in God—until they rest in the gracious one who is their true home. Since 1973, the Shalem Institute has formed hundreds of spiritual groups that provide an environment to encourage our realization of our true home in God and to foster our desire to live out of that home moment by moment. Over the years, these groups have offered many different ways of helping people appreciate and embrace our divine home and its callings in the present moment, drawing especially on the riches of contemplative tradition.

Since 1978, Shalem has sponsored an extension program for the enrichment of *one-to-one* spiritual companions. Nine years later, a member of the Shalem staff, Sister Rose Mary Dougherty, S.S.N.D., was moved to experiment with facilitating a contemplative *group* form of spiritual direction. Six people committed themselves to gather monthly with her for a year—people who shared a desire for God, a readiness to be prayerfully present for one another as they probed God's Spirit in their daily

1

lives, and a willingness to pray for one another between meetings. The group incorporated a spacious, listening silence at various points in each session. This first experience of group spiritual direction at Shalem was found to be so valuable that its members continued to meet together for many years, rotating the role of facilitator.

Three members of that group (including a co-editor of this book, Lynne Smith) and a number of other people gradually came to work with Rose Mary as facilitators for new groups. These groups have grown to the extent that I have been put out of my office at times in order to give space to one of the groups! Lynne and others of these leaders have helped Rose Mary mount an annual workshop for people interested in exploring what it is to be a facilitator of such groups. In 1995, Rose Mary published a book on the nature and practice of group spiritual direction, *Group Spiritual Direction* (Paulist Press), as well as a video of a group session. In 2000, she and Lynne took a major additional step: the beginning of a national extension program for the development of facilitators of group spiritual direction.

The stories of group spiritual direction in this book are largely written by people who have participated in these workshops and in Shalem groups. These authors relate how they have taken what they learned and adapted it to a great variety of settings, from groups in congregations, a seminary, among the homeless, on Capitol Hill, with clergy groups, and many other places. The moving, positive witness of these groups gives an indication of how valuable they can be, not only for their members, but for what their members in turn bring to their daily lives of listening to the Spirit in other people, in their congregations, families, workplaces, and communities. They witness to a form of authentic, intimate spiritual community and a way of touching into the Spirit's living, guiding presence that can be seen as a Spirit-sensitive foundation for the larger communal life of religious and social institutions.

I believe such groups hold enormous potential value for the renewal and deepening of both individual and communal spiritual life. They are not for everyone, and thus they need to be seen as complementing a variety of other kinds of spiritually oriented small groups, including one-to-one spiritual direction. However, I am convinced that they are meant for many more people than have yet found them. In a significant way, they can help meet the widespread hunger of many people for a safe, challenging, accountable group of spiritual friends with whom to probe the deep mystery of God's presence in the unfolding of their lives over time.

Beyond the practical value of the many varied insights, experiences, and approaches to group spiritual direction shown by the contributors to this unique volume, I was inspired by the thread of contact with the Living Spirit woven through all of their accounts. Collectively they left me affirmed in sensing how close that Spirit is to us and how much we are loved and guided by its light. The groups create an atmosphere that invites a thinning of the wall between our ignorance and our awareness of the Holy Spirit's mysterious, incredible intimacy within and among us, closer than our breath. When members of a group sense this same Spirit as the living ground of each person and of the group's movements, then the truest kind of spiritual community appears.

> *Tilden Edwards*
> Founder and Senior Fellow
> Shalem Institute for Spiritual Formation
> Bethesda, Maryland

Introduction

Rose Mary Dougherty, S.S.N.D.

This book had its beginning several years ago, though I didn't realize it at the time. Lynne Smith and I offered what we called "A Refresher in Group Spiritual Direction" for people who had been in touch with us after the annual Group Spiritual Direction Workshops to tell us about their spiritual direction groups at home. Twenty of us gathered for four days. We began our time with storytelling, people taking turns relating what drew them into offering group spiritual direction, their experiences of doing this, how they prayed about it, and what they had learned from their experience. After all the stories were told, we moved to sharing our questions and our wonderings about next steps for group spiritual direction in our at-home settings. The members of the group became resources for one another.

Lynne and I left that gathering with a heightened appreciation for the work people are doing in group spiritual direction and for its potential for transforming lives. We began to pray and dialogue about how we might best replicate the experience of the refresher for a larger audience so that others also might share our appreciation. Out of our prayer came the inspiration for this book and for Shalem's program, Facilitating Group Spiritual Direction.

As Lynne and I prayed about who might be right to contribute to this book, we realized there were many viable options. We narrowed our options to two groups of people. First, we were looking for people to represent the variety of settings in which group spiritual direction was being offered. Our hope was that together their essays would offer a collage of rich possibilities in which you might get a glimpse of your own unique setting and calling. Second, we were looking for people who seemed to have a grasp of the underpinning of group spiritual direction and who could articulate their experiential knowledge of some of its foundational elements. We chose people who could write about intercessory prayer, silence, or spiritual community.

Our theologies may differ from those the writers convey, and we may not necessarily agree with the alterations some have introduced into the process of group spiritual direction. In our Shalem program for Facilitating Group Spiritual Direction, as we mentor facilitators, we might ask them to reflect on how the theology they are conveying reflects their experience of God. In other cases, we might ask how they sense the process honors the primary intent of group spiritual direction.

Taken as a whole, however, these essays reflect the variations that can find a home in the process of group spiritual direction. The process at its best allows for different theologies, spiritualities, personalities, and styles of facilitation. Yet any authentic process of group spiritual direction will always be based on the same essential qualities we look for in participants:

- A shared desire for God;
- A reverence for the uniqueness of the Spirit's manifestation in each person; and
- A willingness to be prayerfully present for one another during the time in the group and to pray for one another outside the group.

We are grateful for all the people who have contributed to the completion of this book. It is truly "the work of many hands" and the fruit of much prayerful support. It has brought together a community of people, many who don't know one another but who share a common appreciation for the value of group spiritual direction. We offer this book to you in the hope that it will:

- Deepen your understanding of the process of group spiritual direction;
- Nourish your creativity as you imagine the setting in which you or others might offer group spiritual direction;
- Support your own discernment as you pray about the rightness of offering group spiritual direction.

As you pray about the rightness of facilitating group spiritual direction, it may be helpful to consider what your role would and would not be with the group. Your primary role as facilitator is to assist the group in being faithful to its common task—being present to God for one another and offering the fruit of that presence as it is called forth. In the beginning, you may need to model both the process and the kinds of conversation appropriate to the process. Equally important, however, will be your encouragement for group members to assume responsibility for the prayerful listening and discernment that happens in the group.

You are not there as the spiritual director for the group. If you think you are, then that could get in the way of being a good facilitator; you may want to assume too much responsibility for the group. In order to be a good facilitator you need:

- Trust in the Spirit's presence through the process;
- Some experience of the process (this can be gained through a colleague group for spiritual directors that uses a process similar to that of group spiritual direction, or from a group of peers who gather for group spiritual direction and rotate the facilitation);
- An appreciation for the intent and dynamic of spiritual direction (if you have never been in one-to-one spiritual direction, you may find it helpful to do that as a means of cultivating your understanding of spiritual direction and for support in your discernment of call).

As you pray about the rightness of your calling, the following questions might assist you:

- What's going on in your life right now that played a part in your attraction to this book?

- What drew you to the book?

- As you read the book, what seems to shimmer for you?

- What resonates with your experience? What do you question? What do you want to explore through other means?

- What does the book seem to say to you in terms of your own sense of calling to become involved in group spiritual direction? How might you pray about this? Who might support you in your discernment around this sense of calling?

There are times when I wonder if my conviction about the value of group spiritual direction has subtly eased over into attachment. I suspect there may be some truth in this. Perhaps that is why some of the work on this book has been so difficult. Yet I cannot deny my own experience or the experience of so many others who speak of the gift group spiritual direction has been in their lives. I suspect that God is doing some transforming, some detaching in me as I write this. I pray that God might use my efforts, my frustrations, even my attachments for you, the reader, for whatever God might want for you as you read the book.

Finally, I want to say that this book is meant to supplement, not replace, my first book, *Group Spiritual Direction: Community for Discernment*, published by Paulist Press in 1995, and a video by the same name produced in 1997. For those of you who have never participated in group spiritual direction, I

am including an outline from the book of the process and guidelines for participants. However, I want to make clear that these
will only make sense against the backdrop of my understanding
of the underpinnings of group spiritual direction: spiritual community, intercessory prayer, and the silence of listening. The last
section of this book contains several essays dealing with these
topics. Once again, however, I would point you to the book,
Group Spiritual Direction: Community for Discernment, for an
extended discussion of these.

The Process of Group Spiritual Direction

The process best happens in a group with four people, five max-
imum and three minimum, all of whom are seeking spiritual
direction and are willing to enter into a process where spiritual
direction can happen for themselves and the others in the group.
Initially, this willingness as well as the match of the group for
each person will need to be tested. Prospective members will
need to pray together and then talk about their understandings
of spiritual direction and what it is in their lives with God that
makes them think this group would be right for them. Diversity
of faith perspectives in the group can enrich the collective wisdom available through the group process.

There should be sufficient time for participants to become
acquainted with one another at a faith level and to become
somewhat familiar with the faith language of one another
before actually beginning the group direction. This time is
especially important for groups comprised of friends or persons

frequently together in other settings. Such groups might benefit also from the presence of an outside facilitator in the beginning. Once a group has decided that it wants to be together for spiritual direction, then it might agree to meet for ten months to a year, and after a review of its time, continue for another year if it seems right.

A two-and-a-half-hour meeting time allows a spaciousness for the unfolding of the process of group spiritual direction. A period longer than two and a half hours seems to tax most people's listening capacity. Four- or five-week intervals between meetings honor that sacred space within each person where ultimately all discernment happens and yet allows for a continuity in the group's life together. If a group can meet biweekly, six members would be optimum to allow for the participation of all members, with three people sharing one week and a different three the next week.

The Process

The time begins with a silent gathering of about twenty minutes for people to gather their hearts into a common desire for God and to dedicate the evening for our world. After the silence, the facilitator invites someone to begin sharing when he or she feels ready.

Sharing by One Person (10 to 15 minutes)

While individuals are sharing, the group listens prayerfully through to the end without interruption.

Silence (3 to 4 minutes)

This silence is simply a time for making space for God, for allowing God to cut through the limits of biases and accustomed ways of responding so that individuals might respond to the presenter from a place of freedom.

Response (about 10 minutes)

The response period provides time for sharing the questions or comments that have come up in the silence. The facilitator might need to encourage trust of God's caring love for the presenter, active in the silence and in the words. This trust is honored when individuals listen to the response of others and move with the flow of the group instead of holding on to a personal agenda for the person.

Silence (about 5 minutes)

During this time, people pray for the person who has just presented. The presenter may want to take some notes on what she has heard.

> *The "Sharing—Silence—Response —Silence"*
> *is repeated, with a short break midway,*
> *until all members have presented.*

Prayer for Absent Member (at least 10 minutes)

This prayer reflects the belief that the most important thing members can do for one another is to pray. Not only does the group pray for the person who cannot be present, but members also are asked to pray for one another in whatever way is right for them outside the time of the group.

Reflection on the Time Together (about 10 minutes)

This reflection is not meant to analyze the time together or to control future outcomes. Instead, it is a gentle looking and noticing, God and the group together, and an honest sharing around what is seen. The focus for this time is the sense of prayerfulness within the group and within individuals. Whatever is addressed—silence, words, the human dynamics within the group—is viewed in terms of that prayerfulness, what has served it or has gotten in its way.

The following questions may be helpful in this reflection:

- How prayerful were we during this session? What was the quality of our silence? Our attention to God? What seemed to take us from attention to God?

- How well did we stay focused on the spiritual life of each person, on the God-relationship beneath the content of what people presented? Where did we get off course?

- Were there places where we got "off track" (for example, doing too much problem solving, being too analytical or philosophical, sharing our own experiences during another's time when it wasn't called for)?

- When I was the directee, was I vulnerable, willing to share what seemed to be called for? Was I open to hearing what others had to say to me? Were there times when the words of another seemed to interrupt or get in the way of my discernment? Is there any feedback I need to give people about this?

- As a listener for the others, where did my words or my silence seem to be coming from? A place of trust? A place of competition? My need to feel superior to others or appear learned? Am I willing simply to offer a question, an idea, or an image to a person for his or her consideration and then let go of it, or do I keep on pushing it? Do I listen to the questions of others, or do I hold on to my agenda for the person?

- Is there any particular awareness or prayer that I take from our time together? Any particular way I would like the group to pray for me?

Guidelines for Group Members

- Pray for others in the group and for the group as a whole between sessions in whatever way is right for you.

- Be consistent in whatever practice seems best to reflect and honor your unique relationship with God at this time, perhaps journaling about what you perceive, sense, or want concerning your attention to God and the way God seems to be dealing with you in all facets of your life. It could be helpful to notice things like:

  —Your desire for God, your desire to desire God;

  —The persons and circumstances that seem to draw you to God or connect you to God or to the meaning or the hope for your life;

—The way you sense God involved in your life, your
resistance to God or areas where you shut out God,
and so forth.

- Before coming to the group, spend time in prayer,
reflecting on your prayer and your journaling since the
last meeting, asking for a sense of what is to be shared.
Allow for the possibility that something entirely different
may show itself in the actual moment of your sharing.

- Come as early for the group as you wish, but be prepared
to start on time. Since some people might be using the
room for prayer before you arrive, please enter the room
in silence. (Those who want to socialize before the
group begins can gather in another room.)

- During the time of small group sharing, continue in the
prayerful presence begun in the large group, simply trying to be available to God in whatever way seems good
for you. Try to be considerate of others in the group by
confining your sharing to the allotted time, about
twenty-five minutes per person, including what you
share about yourself and the group's response. Look
upon your time of sharing as a time for you to talk about
your God-relationship as you are experiencing it in all
areas of your life.

- Hold in reverence and confidence what you hear in the
group.

- Honor your commitment to the group by being present for all sessions. But, if you know you are going to be absent, let someone in the group know. If it is possible and you are comfortable doing so, send a note to group members, describing as well as you can what seemed to be going on between you and God during the past month. Perhaps you will be able only to talk about the way you would like people to be praying for you during the month. This will, one hopes, ease your sharing at the next meeting; it may also give a focus for the time of prayer for you during the session and during the rest of the month.

- If circumstances make it impossible for you to continue your participation in the group, return for a final session of closure with the group whenever possible, or, if that is not possible, be in touch with each member of the group.

NOTE: It is well to remember that these are only guidelines to assist us in our common purpose. The most important components of group spiritual direction are our willingness to be intentional about our spiritual journeys in whatever way is most authentic for us now, our prayerful presence and openness to God for one another, and our willingness to share our spiritual journeys with one another.

I.

Choosing Between One-to-One and Group Spiritual Direction

As the interest in group spiritual direction grows, the questions most frequently raised about it are:

- Can spiritual direction really happen in a group setting?
- How do I choose the people who are right for it?
- How do I choose between one-to-one spiritual direction and group spiritual direction for myself or make a recommendation to someone else about this choice?

Consideration of each of these questions is best done with a general understanding of spiritual direction.

17

Spiritual direction is a process in which two people (or a group of people) meet on a regular basis in an atmosphere of prayer to pay attention to the undercurrents of the Spirit being manifested in the life of one of the participants at that time. It is a way of honoring our desire to live from the core of our being, the place where we are truly ourselves, where we are one with all. Thus, spiritual direction is meant to be a vehicle of discernment, fostering the awareness of the congruence or incongruence between our soul desires and our daily choices.

Here are some questions for those considering spiritual direction:

- Do I want God? Do I want to live my life in intentional relation to ultimate reality? Truth? Goodness? Do I want my life to reflect this wanting?

- Am I willing to make the choices that will honor this desire and bring it and my choices into greater accord?

- Do I sense it might be helpful to have a companion (companions) in prayer and discernment as I seek to live authentically?

- Am I willing to share my spiritual journey with another (others) through spiritual direction where I will intentionally talk about my journey on a regular basis?

If the answer to these questions is Yes, then the raw material for spiritual direction is present, whether in a one-to-one setting or a group, provided all involved are committed to prayer for one another and the groundedness of prayer during their time together.

A person considering group spiritual direction also might ask:

- Do I sense the invitation to learn from the spiritual journeys of others?

- Am I willing to be in a prayerful listening place for others, to be a companion in prayer and discernment?

- Do I sense the Spirit can be present in theologies and spiritualities different from mine? Am I open to hearing of different theologies and spiritualities?

- Do I trust that the Spirit can be present for me through other members of the group?

- Am I willing to commit to the group process?

There are other considerations for someone trying to choose between one-to-one spiritual direction and group spiritual direction, starting with the obvious questions:

- What happens when I try to pray about this?

- What sense do I get about what might be called for now?

There might also be the very practical issue of one's schedule. Someone who travels a lot or who has numerous responsibilities may find it easier to coordinate a schedule with one other person on a month-to-month basis than with a group, usually for several months in advance.

Rose Mary Dougherty

It may also be helpful to look at questions such as:

- Do I have a tendency to hide behind other people in a group, listening to others but seldom sharing what might be given me for sharing?

- How possible would it be for me to be just a member of the group and not responsible for it? Am I so often in a leadership position that I might gravitate toward that in this setting?

- Do I often find myself in competition with others in a group setting, perhaps trying to impress them with my learning or experience?

- Am I too upset right now to really be able to listen to others? Am I apt to usurp others' time by relating everything they say back to my own issues? Do I see any evidence of this in my daily conversations now?

- If I were to choose one-to-one direction, might I give too much authority to the director? Might I be so self-conscious that it would be difficult for me to be myself?

- In which form of spiritual direction do I sense I might have the greater interior freedom to be in a prayerful listening place as I seek to pay attention to God in my life?

Obviously, group spiritual direction will not be right for everyone who is called to be in spiritual direction, nor will it be right for anyone all the time. Ideally, people considering group spiritual direction will have sufficient interior freedom, self-knowledge, and sense of the process of group spiritual direction to make a discerning decision about the rightness of the group for them. There are times, however, when the decision must fall to a facilitator or to those who are coordinating a program of group spiritual direction. The questions posed for people considering group spiritual direction may also be used by those who must screen applicants. There is no easy way to do this, but experience confirms that not everyone who would like to be in group spiritual direction is right for it. Consideration must be given not only to the individual but also to those with whom we are making a commitment when we accept them for group spiritual direction. Ultimately, one must trust that the same Spirit who seems to be present in a decision to refuse an applicant will be there for the applicant as well. We cannot know how God will use our decision, even if it be erroneous, for the other. The best we can do is bring our decision to prayer, being willing to be available to God for the other. This, after all, is the heart of spiritual direction itself.

Rose Mary Dougherty

Reflections on an Eight-Year Journey

Tom Adams, Ken Clansky,
Rosemary Eyre-Brook, and Anne Lipe

Four people praying together regularly for eight years is a profound and potentially life-changing experience. For the four of us, it has been that and more. We've had the privilege—perhaps better described as a blessing or grace—to be in group spiritual direction together for eight years. None of us had long-term intentions when we tentatively signed up. We come from quite varied backgrounds and probably never would have met but for this experience.

Spiritual growth is a beautiful but at times lonely and scary trip. Group spiritual direction has transformed and blessed each of us and supported us through major life changes and the challenges of everyday life. We've shared personal struggles—recovery from addictions, career changes, business dilemmas, and marital and parenting challenges. While the sharing of real-life experiences is important, it's difficult to put in words what really happens in group spiritual direction. During the eight years, we've prayed together, shared our spiritual journeys, and seen interior and exterior change in each other.

This essay tries to capture something about the unique form of spiritual intimacy called group spiritual direction. We will try to share how coming together once a month as a group, and as part of a larger group direction community, has impacted our lives. Together, we have been invited into simple yet profound questions such as "Where am I right now in relation to God? What's going on between God and me? Where is God in this experience?" We'll attempt to describe how this process has allowed us to be with—and to understand—God in new ways. We'll also explore how being with God through silence and mutual prayer has allowed us to experience the power of silence and of praying together over the questions.

What follows is our collective story of who we are, why we came together, what we've experienced, and why we've stayed together as a spiritual direction group. We hope it's useful to you; reflecting on this experience has been a blessing for us.

Four Individual Journeys Converge

We were led to group spiritual direction by different paths. Ken is a partner in a small business, married with four children, and a convert to Roman Catholicism. His spiritual hunger caused him to enroll in two different theology programs in the mid-1980s, where he was exposed to different forms of prayer and heard about spiritual direction. "I didn't know how to find a spiritual director, was curious if it might help me, yet too reserved to ask, so I decided to sign up for the group spiritual direction program at Shalem."

Anne is a music therapist with a background in both vocal and piano training. For her, the arts have always been a special window into the heart of God. In 1988, she encountered a film character who had a powerful impact on her spiritual journey. The film's story was familiar, the character a legendary one, but there were surprising twists that allowed archetypal images and meanings to come to life. The character's own journey toward awareness and his struggles to realize the fullness of his humanity stirred something deep within Anne's soul. "It was as if God threw open a door to an inner chamber and allowed sunlight to illumine the depths of my heart." She began to journal about her experience and found herself in dialogue with this character. "I've always had an active imagination, which I frequently try to shove aside, but this was exactly the part of me that God was trying to reach. I was not at all sure where God was headed with all of this, but I trusted the process. Through these journal dialogues, I learned a great deal about myself, my prayer life, scripture, and God's presence in my life experience. I also discovered the writings of the mystics and eventually learned about spiritual direction. As a Lutheran, I had not been exposed to either."

In 1991, she discovered Shalem and attended an arts and spirituality quiet day. "The atmosphere of silence and the encouragement to be aware of the inner movements of God's Spirit within seemed most congruent with the teachings that had emerged over the years of my journaling. At this point in my life, I felt a need to externalize my experience, to get beyond my early morning coffee and dialogue about what God seemed to be up to in my life. I was drawn to the idea of a community and the opportunity to share my journey with fellow seekers."

Rosemary grew up as an Anglican in England and experienced her first spiritual awakening at confirmation. She seriously considered becoming a missionary and instead spent a year in Zambia with the British equivalent of the American Peace Corps and then became a doctor. Arriving in the United States and having four children in four and a half years, church attendance wasn't nourishing her spirit. She found Shalem and took a contemplative prayer course. At the end of the second year, the leaders asked participants to explore what might be next on their spiritual journey. "Group or one-to-one spiritual direction was suggested among the options, so I decided to give group direction a try."

Tom came to the group reluctantly, by way of individual direction. Raised Catholic, and having spent high school and college in the seminary, he was familiar with individual spiritual direction. After reconnecting with the church of his youth through twelve-step spirituality, he began to work with a spiritual director. "I had three different directors over a four- to six-year period when I was in my mid-thirties. I was married with three children and worked with a network of community development organizations. I liked the attention and direct feedback from individual direction."

Tom's last individual director was familiar with group spiritual direction. She encouraged him to pray about whether group direction was right for him. "Reluctantly I agreed to give the group experience a try. I was really worried that the messages from God would become less clear and I would lose some of the individual attention to my unique needs. I also had the bias that people with a religious vocation could help me more than regular lay people. All these fears eventually proved groundless."

Our Early Experience

We initially came to group direction at different times. Tom was part of a facilitated group for a year and met Anne in that group. Two members of the group didn't return the next year, and Rosemary and Ken joined the group with Anne and Tom.

Rosemary describes her early experience this way: "Tom and Anne had already been in a group and appeared to know what group direction was all about. Ken found talking easy, but I did not. It felt very risky opening up to the group, but when I did, I knew I was held in God's love. I felt intimidated to respond to others' sharing—how would I know that it was from God and not just my own ego? But I was drawn to the group. I loved the silence and the space to let God be God."

Initially, Ken found the notion of people praying together in silence foreign. He had never experienced anything like it before. "Getting through the first few group spiritual direction sessions was not easy for me. It was a new process with new people, and I was not very comfortable with it. About halfway through the first year, it began to feel more natural as I gained an understanding of what group spiritual direction is and is not and as I began to know the members of the group."

Our group transitioned from a facilitated group in two phases. After a year with a facilitator, Tom was asked to serve as facilitator. "I was nervous about this change, too. I was afraid I'd be so worried about the group I wouldn't be present to the process myself. In reality, it helped me realize the importance of relying on God more and not taking my role or myself quite so seriously. All the other members understood the process by then, so my role was mostly timekeeper and initiator of process reflection time at the end of each session."

In Tom's work life, facilitators of group process were much more active. But in group spiritual direction, "the real facilitator is God working through the members. We were blessed initially by an experienced Shalem facilitator, who modeled for us how to be with each other prayerfully without problem solving or being intrusive. Her example made it possible for us to become a self-facilitated group several years later."

In the second phase, our group moved to self-facilitation. We recognized that we were all equally capable of serving as facilitator and that the role of facilitator had become fairly minor. During the next several years, we evolved from taking turns as facilitator (keeping time and initiating the process discussion at the end) to a process where there is no formal timekeeper and periodically one of us suggests that we have a process discussion at the end.

Anne sums up our early experience this way: "What drew me to this process was the sense of community—having an opportunity to share with fellow seekers. And there was mutuality. I was invited to share my stories, issues, and questions about my life with God and to listen for the Spirit's guidance revealed through others. However, I also was invited to listen to others' stories and to prayerfully help others see, hear, and touch God's presence in their life situations. This kind of process attracted me, though it took a while for me and all of us to begin to see its power and to be comfortable with it."

How Group Direction Has Touched Us

Individual Awakenings

Several of us were touched deeply by a few words from our Shalem facilitator in our first year together. "She broke through some 'baggage' I had carried for a long time," Ken recalls. "Namely, my belief that I had to get my life in order before I could be worthy of God's love. In a drafty church basement, by candlelight one winter's night, she passionately challenged me about God's unconditional and very personal love, a love independent of my worthiness. I'll never forget the message, the passion with which it was delivered, or the unusual setting."

For Tom, the memory of the same incident is the words: "'God is so in love with you'—they were burnt into my consciousness in a way I can never forget. When I doubt or am down or am sharing with a friend who hasn't accepted God's love or doubts it for the moment, I tap into that experience. Through her words, God's love for us came alive."

Rosemary also remembers that night. "There have been many times when I have dragged myself to group spiritual direction and shared my self-doubts and struggles with prayer only to have Tom remind me of God's infinite, unconditional love for me. Then I have known why I came."

Another incident that has stayed with Tom also occurred in his early experience. "One of the members was struggling with her tendency to doubt herself and doubt God. She shared about the Bible story of Lot looking back and turning into salt. I had heard the story hundreds of times. That night, the way she described it, it struck me and gave me a lifelong image of how doubting hardens me and drains me of life."

Big Decisions

Rosemary brought a number of big career decisions to our group. "The group and the Spirit working in the group have guided me through a number of very difficult career decisions. In my career restlessness, I first decided to do a difficult year as a fellow in pediatric anesthesia, part of a longer, ongoing struggle of whether or not to give up the practice of medicine. Through this process, I've been led to enroll in a masters of theology program at a local seminary. The journey is still unfolding; I know I can bring the ups and downs and clarity and confusion to group prayer and indeed more is eventually revealed. I find acceptance and the incarnation of God's love in the group that sustains me in the 'not knowing' of the journey."

One of the big issues that Anne has dealt with over the years is "integration." When she began group direction, she was in the process of completing a doctoral program in human growth and development. "Somehow, I had this notion that those magic letters (Ph.D.) would open the door to a fulfilling vocation (i.e., a full-time job). The group consistently was able to flesh out ways in which that integration already was present, ways in which God already was opening doors and using my gifts and desires for others. Tom is always reminding me how much God wants good for me in all things. The good is present in God's self, God's presence. This is what integrates my life, not the external structure that I think should be there."

Tom's personal struggles were often a part of his sharing, too. "I often didn't know what to do. I had tried everything I knew. Through the quiet and prayer together, the path became clear. Once I made a decision, unlike many other decisions, I wasn't tortured by doubt and second-guessing. I truly believe that God's hand was somehow guiding me."

Ken has struggled for years with a difficult business situation and partnership relationship, for which there has seemed to be no satisfactory resolution. "The group has supported me in this long-term problematical situation but has also continually challenged me to open myself to God where I am now and not to see God only in my own ideas for a happy outcome. In other words, group spiritual direction supports us at a deeper level than the particular circumstances and difficulties that form the terrain of our lives and through that deeper connection influences decisions we make about our lives."

Tom Adams, Ken Clansky, Rosemary Eyre-Brook, and Anne Lipe

Appreciating Silence

Each of us had different reactions to the notion of sitting in silence together. "Early in the process," Anne explains, "I recall being struck by the emphasis which was placed on silence. The evening's darkness, the small candle illuminating the room and the prayerfulness of the opening time with the larger group has helped carry me further into silence as we gathered for our small group time. There always has been a freedom, a special invitation in this silence. It's as if during my time of sharing, my story is gently, lovingly received. The silence allows time for reflection, for me to try to clarify aspects of my story for the group and for myself. I've learned that there is power in group silence. Occasionally it feels as though we are doing nothing together. I'm frequently ready to get things started, but God invites me deeper into this 'doing nothing as a group' place for a reason. This corporate sense of receptivity to God is a very precious thing not to be rushed through."

Rosemary began her adjustment through her earlier Shalem experiences in which silence also was emphasized. "I felt nurtured and accepted. I grew in my understanding of God and myself. The peace and the silence felt like home. While I was anxious about what to say, I was drawn to the group and the silence. It created a space to let God be God. I felt grounded, loved and restored and came away with a better perspective on life."

For Tom, sitting still was a challenge. "By the time I got to group direction, I had improved. Sitting still for five or ten minutes wasn't impossible. I spent a lot of nights squirming and wanting there to be more action. At times I still feel this way."

Spiritual Deepening and Growth

Rosemary sums it up for all of us in her unique, to-the-point way: "Over time I grew and found my voice. I also learned to be a better listener for God and to let God use my voice. This has been helped by knowing that I am being held up to God through the group's prayers, that the group is listening to my heart for God and not trying to fix me. In my private prayer time over the years in the group, I've experienced both closeness to and, sometimes, distance from God. Through it all, my faith and capacity to trust God and God's leadings in me has grown. That's a lot of change."

"For me, one of the greatest benefits to staying together for a number of years is witnessing very intimately the spiritual path of the other group members," Tom adds. "As I watch others take risks in changing their prayer practice or go through their version of the 'dark night of the soul' and come out of it with more faith, I can't help but have more faith in God and God's mysterious work in all our lives. For me, Anne is a spiritual pioneer whose path I often can relate to and watch closely. I grow and am inspired as I prayerfully watch. As a result, words in books about spiritual development come alive and have faces."

Learning to listen is another gift of this process. "In group direction," Anne explains, "I've learned how to listen prayerfully, to listen with a sense of openness to God's spirit. This is quite different from casual, conversational listening in which

I'm more focused on how the other person's words make me feel or on forming an argument to what the person is saying. I've learned in group direction that it is okay to be aware of how my feelings respond to someone's sharing, but those feelings are filtered through my prayerful attentiveness to God. I listen for the Spirit's desire for the person that may be present in those feelings. For me, the silence provides the freedom to listen, to pray, to be."

Individual Gifts

As would be expected, we are four very different personalities. The mix adds to the texture and richness of the experience. Ken listens with a deep, analytical heart and mind, and hears and remembers details of our journeys that we've often forgotten. He builds his case and introduces his ideas in great detail—at times a challenge to some in the group.

Others recall Rosemary's early days in the group, how she seemed reluctant to offer questions or guidance for others. It has been a gift to share in her blossoming and growing confidence in her ability to listen to God for herself and others. Her guidance always feels "to the point." She seems to be able to go to the heart of an issue.

Tom was comfortable in the realm of the Spirit early on and often adds a poetic touch to his sharing. Anne likes to summarize with images, as does Ken. Between them, they create vivid pictures of the sharing.

Process Reflections and Ongoing Assessment

Reflecting on something you value deeply can lead to an overly positive recollection or romanticization. We hope we've not succumbed to that. In our reflection together about these eight years, we've shared the many evenings we didn't want to come, the questions of some of us about whether to continue, and our spoken and unspoken worries and concerns. Here are some of them that might be useful to groups:

- Our group evolved. We had fears and doubts about having a facilitator from among the group, and again when we went to having no facilitator and sharing the responsibilities. Over time, it always worked out, largely by talking about our goals and by being open.

- We find it important to go over the basic principles regularly, at least annually. We find we can "forget" to pray for each other or become sloppy about having a "process time" at the end of each session. Regular check-ins help us with this.

- It has felt important to us to meet at the same time and place as other group spiritual direction groups, and it has helped our group in a number of ways. First, it has helped create an atmosphere of prayerfulness in a community setting larger than the four of us. Coming together in a larger group for quiet at the outset of the evening supports the transition from everyday busyness to a prayerful presence. Finally, being a part of the larger community has helped us with our individual and collective accountability. We're reminded by others why we are there and what the time is about.

- Over the years, we've experienced occasional absences, and for a year, one of our members was working in another community and was unable to come. We suspect that absences are less disruptive over time. When our one member was away, we prayed for her and felt her presence. Occasionally when only two of us can come, there is more of a conversational quality and less of a group prayerfulness experience. The advantage of our group's longevity (even when one or two of us is absent) is that the room feels filled up with prayer and there is a sense of the greater "communion of saints" that we are all partaking in.

- There have certainly been evenings when we have not been able to settle in the silence and have made shopping lists, worried, or almost fallen asleep. But even then, each of us has felt the gift of the group's acceptance.

- In our previous meeting space, the rattle of pipes, the noise in the room above us and the outside traffic could all be major distractions, but at times they were strangely comforting.

Final Words

Rosemary sums it up succinctly this way: "Group spiritual direction is a haven and a lifeline. As a haven, it provides me with real time and space to be with God in the presence of like-minded, God-centered people in community. It is a lifeline because it reels me in to God, especially at times when I have drifted far out to sea. I wish I could say that I always pray, but I can't. I can be faithful for months and then be captured by the rush of the world. Group spiritual direction helps shorten my absences and reminds me of what I already know—the importance and centrality of my relationship with God in all I do in this life. As a member of this small community, I am committed to being honest to the other members of the group and to myself. Their loving presence as fellow travelers enables me to strive to do this."

There Is a River...

Gordon Forbes

I knew an ending was at hand and "handing over" was in the offing when I began writing memoirs of the four churches I had served for more than forty years. In February 1999, I announced my intention to retire from the pastorate of my church at the end of October.

The writing of those memoirs became a two-edged sword in my life. On the one hand, it was deeply satisfying. My mind filled with faces of beloved people, milestones of achievement, experiences, both painful and pleasing, that forced me to grow. My life overflowed with a sense of gratitude and grace. A silent, invisible, beneficent presence had accompanied me in my life.

On the other hand, I sensed all the potential losses facing me in this handing over of responsibility. Euphoria sets in for all of us when we first think of retirement. All our unfulfilled fantasies swell us with hope and excitement. Only as the time approaches do the realities of change hit us.

My apprehension grew. What would life be like? Would I really be able to do what I wanted? I sensed freedom would not only be a gift but a challenge. Was I up to it?

Two tensions asserted themselves as the retirement date approached. One was the tension between professional and personal life. I had spent such energy in professional performance—calling on people, relating to community concerns, preaching at least forty sermons a year, managing staff, teaching classes, administering an institution, responding to crises of various kinds. None of those responsibilities would be operative any longer. When a professional ministry is over, a vocation still remains. What was the new call? How would I discern it?

A second tension surfaced—the tension between community and isolation. One of my children once said the coolest thing about being a minister's kid was the presence of instant community wherever you moved. It's true. Community is given to ministers and their families, for better or worse. However, my denomination requires a complete severing of ties with a congregation once you retire. How would I deal with isolation and the need for new community? An old hymn sustained me in this time:

> *Guide me, O Thou Great Jehovah*
> *Pilgrim in this barren land.*
> *I am weak but Thou art mighty,*
> *Hold me with Thy powerful hand.*
> *Bread of Heaven, Bread of Heaven*
> *Feed me now and evermore*
> *Feed me now and evermore.*

The flyer from the Shalem Institute came in the mail early one July day, announcing group spiritual direction. A vague feeling told me I should do it. I had participated in various Shalem programs. Despite my action-driven life, part of me has a thirst for the meditative—up to a point. So I applied.

Groups are very familiar to me. I have participated in scores of them—sensitivity groups, therapy groups, skill-enhancing groups, training and empowerment groups. Most of them have been "talk" or "experiential learning" groups. They have concentrated on skills—learning new ones and improving learned ones. They have been heavy on practical work, psychological insights, and combinations of confrontation and comfort. None of them gave more than lip service to prayer. They trusted in the adequacy of human perception. Something told me that simple human perception was not going to hold me up this time.

My first group spiritual direction meeting at Shalem was incredible. It began with a considerable amount of silence, fostering centering down into God. No introductions or group building: the telling of names, the reporting of "what you do," or what goals you had for this program. The introductions came *after* the silence and were minimal. More silence followed, with a brief meditation by a "facilitator."

The whole emphasis focused on one thing: *What goes on between God and us individually and collectively?* It required contemplation, not interaction. The power came not only in personal, inward meditation but also in intercession, holding each other in prayer, a major emphasis of all contemplative practice. To gather together in communal prayer and discernment can break any sense of isolation and provide a spiritual connection that is gentle and pervasive. It creeps into the individual like fog, filling up the nooks and crannies of separate existence without reliance on words. It also is a safeguard against the delusions possible in an over-individualized practice.

The program was explained. We would break into groups of four, each group with its own facilitator. We would begin with prayer. Someone would then share from his or her life for ten minutes, followed by more silence and prayer focusing on "Where do you see God in this?" Ten minutes of response from the other members of the group would be followed by more prayer. Then, after all had gone through this discipline, the group would end with some reflections on the process and how we saw the presence of the Spirit working in the room. We would leave pledged to intercession for each other in the days between meetings.

I wondered if this was for me. I thought I needed harder stuff, like confrontation. I could handle conflict and controversy, but here I was being called to trust this gentle, seemingly passive, highly introspective way. I suspended all judgment and plunged in like a rookie.

It proved exciting and perplexing. I entered a gentle whirlpool that started more like a soft current in our first small group meeting. Several group members faced circumstances that required a letting go. Two of us needed to let go of an adult child; another wanted to let go of the fear of letting go, of losing individual freedom. In the silence after each sharing, a common image emerged from our prayer for each other: God seemed to be calling us to let the river of his love carry us. The river image

Gordon Forbes

spoke to each of us powerfully. That month, between meetings,
I had visited Harper's Ferry, West Virginia, on the first day of my
retirement. It has always held a strange attraction for me. This
poem emerged as a result of that visit.

Down Stream

I watch thirty ninth-graders
board the shuttle—field trip to the National Park.
They will learn of Union and Confederate
maneuvers, hear of cannon, rifles, and insurrection.

But I will ignore this history now.
I feel pulled toward the river
to a rock at the spot
where legs of two rivers meet.

The wind peels leaves,
just past peak, twirls them
to rushing currents. River
receives their fluttering, carries them
downstream. Rocks, and whirlpools
ahead, the tumble over Great Falls,
headed for the bay. Conception,
birth, death converge.

The white spire of St. Peter's church
juts like a needle above the trees,
points to heaven. But I have not come

> for heaven. I come to watch the leaves,
> just past peak, get carried away to
> places they cannot imagine on
> this first day of my retirement.

This river image remains, for me, a call to let go and let God. It is a call to trust.

Near the middle of our year in group spiritual direction, another image emerged for us. A member brought in a quote that had spoken deeply to him of the ever-present Spirit in our lives, one to whom we could turn at any moment, even in the midst of a crowded room or a relational conflict. The quote presented us with the possibility of opening to Spirit in the simplest, commonest, even daily, way. It made it clear to me that *retirement* is the wrong word to define my life. Other "re-" words occurred to me, such as *renewal, redirection, reconstruction, even rebirth.* Spirit-given possibilities live all around us.

As we prayed and meditated over the quote, each of us discovered individual ways in which we could open to these Spirit-given possibilities. For one, it meant checking critical and judgmental reactions to things she didn't understand. To another it meant picking up on a relationship that had shriveled over the years.

Such awareness has sensitized me to places where my gifts can be offered. I now teach writing at a dinner program for homeless women. I have made a deepened commitment to my own writing and to finding ways of empowering clergy in becoming contemplative leaders for the years ahead.

Two great paradoxes have emerged in this process. I often reflect on how, at the same time, blessings reveal a level of regret in life. The slow work of trust reveals the foolishness of the obsessive ways we drive ourselves to achieve things that are already given. I count it a blessing to see how available one can actually be for Spirit-led acts and a regret that we miss so many of those opportunities. Our group overflowed with examples of ways the Spirit had led them to be compassionate, gentle, and just at the same time.

More personally, I also see how the blessing of vocation gets overlooked in the practice of professional ministry. I find it generally true that ministers are often the last to plunge into spiritual depths. Handling holy things can sometimes immunize us to the holy in our midst.

The biggest blessing of my year has been participating in group spiritual direction. Two realities stay with me in this process. The core focus question—*Where is God in this?*—surfaces at the most appropriate times, bringing a certain serenity and trust with it and unexpected discernment. The experience of intercession and prayer for and with others creates a bond and gentle power that fill me with a sense of being part of a community that transcends all boundaries. So, I have signed up for a second year.

Individual and Group Spiritual Direction: A Comparison

James Kennedy

In this essay I describe how spiritual direction, both individual and group, has helped me realize the "Spirit" behind my actions; how I came to find a spiritual director, and then later, a group for spiritual direction; and I compare some of the differences in my experience between the two. I also describe some of the ways that God has been with me through this process and what that has meant in practical terms for living my life each day.

Solitude and Reflection

Holy Cross Monastery sits on a 1,000-acre farm in the Shenandoah Valley, with rolling hills grazed by cows owned by nearby farmers who rent the land from the monks. To the east of the property are the Appalachian Mountains, and Snickers Gap (a low point in the Ridge) overlooks the grounds. At the bottom of the ridge, the Shenandoah River meanders in 180-degree turns, a treat for canoeing because you paddle both into and away from the sun.

The river is twenty yards wide, and maybe six feet deep, slow running, and clear so that weeds and river grasses are visible below. The banks are muddy. I go there to watch the river flow by, to look for small mouth bass and sunfish in the shadows of the willows that overhang the river. It's a pleasant place—shaded, not out in the open, lush with water life, plants, and trees.

The first time I went to Holy Cross, I wrote in my journal:

It is my first few minutes [here]. A sense of "what now?" expectation, then boredom, then fear of what might happen, of what God might say to me. It is very quiet and peaceful and no noise but the heater. My room is simple—a bed, a comfortable chair with a reading lamp, a desk built into the wall, and several icons of Christ on the wall. My window overlooks the field where cows graze, and off in the distance is the ridge of mountains that I hiked as a teenager. Driving up the mile-long road to the monastery, I felt the presence of God. Something is definitely different here.

I notice how much I wait for the phone to ring at home and how I wish it were here now so that someone would call. This waiting is always in the back of my mind. I also notice that my regular life is filled with responsibilities and duties and it's impossible to be really centered. I am constantly preoccupied with the next thing to be done—calling a friend, cutting the grass, doing the laundry, etc.

Hints About Spiritual Direction

Other than meals, the monastery has no plans for those who visit. Each person is free to do as he or she wishes—to walk along the Shenandoah River, to sit at the back of the chapel for mass or the hours of the day, to read in the retreat house library. But, every Saturday afternoon, one of the monks makes himself available in a small room in the retreat house for visitors to spend an hour with him simply talking. I signed up, pleased that this unexpected opportunity was here for us and glad that I would have someone with whom to talk.

In the room where we met there was a comfortable easy chair, a small desk with a lamp, and another chair for me. A retired abbot sat directly across from me. After a while, I talked about an Emily Dickinson poem I had read recently at a neighborhood poetry group, how moved I was by it, and how Christian it seemed to me. Poetry in general, and Emily Dickinson in particular, had somehow captured important parts of my faith—the significance of language, the power and mystery inherent in metaphor, the ability to recreate for others the deepest sense of what it is to be human and of God. In the small desk next to my chair, the abbot pulled out a neatly typed sermon of his that centered on a poem by her. I smiled and was drawn to the monks, wished I could have more time with them.

Finding a Director

For a year, I thought occasionally about getting a spiritual director but didn't take any action. A friend and I talked about it. "I want to get one some day," I said.

"Why not call up a monastery?" she asked, as if it were that simple, and it was. I ended up calling a monastery close to where I live. When I called up, I simply asked the question, "Do you do spiritual direction?" and the monk answered that they did. I was to wait for a call from the abbot, and he would set up an interview. After that, he would decide whether they could do it and which monk would meet with me.

Father Abbot agreed to meet, and we went to a room where we sat face to face. An old lamp on an oak table gave off yellow light, and an oriental rug covered the floor. "Well, tell me about yourself. What brought you here tonight?" he asked. I told him that I was looking for help in making a decision. I described my church and how lately I had become disillusioned and confused. I wanted to decide whether to stay or leave. If I stayed, I wanted to understand how I was to participate and be a member of the community. If I left, I wanted to know where to go.

"The church is biblically centered," I said, "a term that in my own practice I embrace but which sometimes means that all answers are known from the Bible." I went on to describe how the church had opened my eyes to the richness of biblical stories and the closeness to God that I could experience through biblical study and meditation.

I was raised Roman Catholic, and Bible study was previously unknown to me. I was moved by the many young people at church who had been in Bible studies and were genuinely wise and loving people. But, more often than not, my study and reflection on the Bible led to more questions and less certainty about particular situations that I faced. After years of study and Bible groups, God seemed to be calling me to another way of relating that was different from the purely "biblically centered" approach in this church. For them, the Bible did have all the answers and enabled them to live contentedly, with a purpose and meaning that I found admirable and longed to have myself. However much I tried, though, this approach did not work for me and did not bring me closer to God.

I was unsure whether my disappointment with the church was something to "work through," "stay with" and pray that I could come to terms with, or whether it was a genuine call from God to move away. I prayed, "God, don't let me leave just because of difficulties, but let me go because you want me to go elsewhere." I prayed these words, yet I felt self-righteous at the same time, believing that my faith was somehow better than theirs. Even though I am a Christian myself, when someone would say, "I am a Christian," I would hear that a wall had been erected between that Christian and others, enclosing the Christians inside, and keeping those on the outside from coming in.

Father Abbot listened intently. At the end of our time together, he said, "I'd like to see you. When can we get together again?" We planned to meet in two weeks, and my homework assignment was to write an autobiography.

Individual Spiritual Direction

My director had been a Benedictine monk for forty years. Each day, the monks meet five times in the chapel to sing psalms and pray, according to the Rule of St. Benedict that was written in the sixth century. Forty years of such practice show, and I have never met anyone like him. He doesn't drive a car, and although he has been urged by many others to write and publish books, he refuses to do so, believing that God has other more immediate things for him to do. As the abbot of the monastery, he is responsible for its operation and for the well-being of the monks. Yet he is also involved in the world. He teaches high school Latin to teenaged boys, and he counsels others like myself. He sees God not just in religious practice and within the walls of the monastery but in many other places.

Gradually I came to realize that Father Abbot has authority. It is not the authority of his simply being a priest or an abbot. He is authoritative for me because he is wiser, closer to God, humbler, and far more loving of people in general than I. I am willing to listen to what he has to say and even to submit at times. This is not the submission that I knew as a child, but a simple recognition that Father Abbot seems closer to God than anyone I have ever met.

A few months after our initial meeting, just before Lent, he was describing what the monastery does for Lent. Each monk gives up something and takes on some new task. All eat less, and they give to the poor the money saved from the meals. One monk gave up his time on the Internet; another spent an extra hour each day in prayer. Father Abbot asked what I was going to give up, a thought that had not occurred to me. I said I didn't know, but then realized that I could volunteer at Joseph's House, a place where homeless men with AIDS lived and were treated well for the last months or years of their lives. Although many of the men got AIDS from drug use and several are gay, there is no judgment about that or desire to convert them. Five years later, I continue to spend time at Joseph's House.

Gradually I left the church I had been attending, staying in touch with the close friends I had made, saying good-bye to the pastor in a lunchtime meeting, but losing contact with acquaintances whom I would see each Sunday. Throughout this transition, Father Abbot was a guide for me—not pulling or pushing me in one particular direction but gently helping, respectful of the choices I had to make. I came to him confused and angry in my relationship with God. I needed a "marriage counselor" and wanted someone who was already married and who knew what a long-lasting, intimate marriage was like. God's prayer for me, brought to me through Father Abbot, was, I believe, to stop seeing God as the one who only provided consolations and tears and to know God in a different, quieter way—the spouse who sits home at nights quietly with me.

James Kennedy

Moving Toward Group Spiritual Direction

As with individual spiritual direction, my coming to group spiritual direction at the Shalem Institute was slow yet seemingly inevitable. Ten years before, a close friend had suggested that I might be interested in finding out more about Shalem and participating in some of Shalem's programs. I went so far as to ask for a brochure, which I read with interest. But Shalem was then located a good hour away from my house. It was the encouragement of a trusted friend who decided to take a workshop at Shalem that eventually caused me to take action.

Shalem had recently moved to just a mile or two from where I work and much closer to my home. I attended a Shalem "sampler"—an evening of learning about the programs for the coming year. Father Abbot and I had been seeing each other less often—there was no specific problem that troubled me any longer, and he had recently been elected to another six-year term as abbot of the monastery and was increasingly busy. Gradually he shifted from spiritual director to spiritual friend, even just friend, which he remains today. But I still longed for times to be intentionally listening to God with others drawn to contemplative practice, and I decided to join group spiritual direction.

Group Spiritual Direction

My first group spiritual direction meeting seemed right—the large group meeting before we broke up into small groups, all of us praying in silence for twenty minutes before anyone spoke.

Although I often pray on my own, my prayers seem to be stronger and more sincere when I'm in the presence of others who are also praying in silence. On my own, my mind drifts into and out of prayer. With others, it is easier to stay focused on prayer, and others' words about God and prayer help me keep my thoughts focused on God.

After our large group meeting, we adjourned to an office for our small group meeting. All five of the people in my first group were strangers. At first, we struggled to learn the process—to be quiet between each others' times for talking, not to give advice, to stay roughly within the time limits for each of us, and to try to hear what God might be saying to us and through us to other people. We had a facilitator who gently helped us with the process.

Many moments in group spiritual direction stand out, but a few more than others. In one, a group member talked about her new job—she had been placed in a new division in the organization, just formed, where it was not yet organized and there was much chaos. The people she worked with were upset, anxious, uncertain about what their place might be, who they would work for, how they would fit in, what the work would be like, and she herself had the same fears. More than that, she struggled with not having any specific work as they organized themselves. She was left to just be in the midst of this reorganization. She was lost because she was so accustomed, as I am, to working and producing and getting the recognition and sense of accomplishment that often comes. At the same time, she thought that God might be telling her to consider where her energy comes from to work—to please others, out of a pure sense of duty—and to consider what she might be doing in this new situation. She noticed that many of her coworkers came to her for comfort or advice, or just to be listened to, and she thought that perhaps this was what God was asking at the moment—not to be so concerned about action and production but to simply be with people. This was so contrary to what she had learned all of her life and, indeed, was contrary to what our culture teaches us.

I recognized myself in her clearly. As I walk into the office each day, I click on a new personality—one of being productive, efficient, businesslike, and devoted to the task at hand. Her struggle is one that I've had my entire life—measuring myself and others by accomplishments. But there is something about this group member's simple honesty and genuine longing to be free of it and open to God in that situation that stays with me. Six months later, I'm still aware in my own work, in my office, of how I am there to comfort others, to produce and be admired for my work, and yet it is still only occasional awareness. I quietly pray, at times, that God let this awareness be transformed into simplicity and sureness that whatever I am doing, or not doing, at work is for God, not for me, and that I face potential failure and rejection.

I also notice how the silence of group spiritual direction makes words and language more significant. I can't say what someone—one person, that is—wants to hear, to feel where they are and please them. There are long periods of silence. When I speak, I notice my tendency to use words to influence others, or to impress, and how difficult it is to say what is deep, personal, and vulnerable.

At one point in our first group, one of the members could not stop talking because she was so upset about some events in her life, but our facilitator gently and firmly called her to stop, to listen, and to take just one of her issues and explore it with the group. I was glad the facilitator was there with us to help bring order and silence again.

Similarities Between Individual and Group Direction

In both types of spiritual direction, all of us had a deep sense of searching for God and wanting to know how God might be present in the situations of our lives.

Whether explicit or not, all of us in spiritual direction recognize that we cannot do it alone, that we need others to hear what we might be saying, to speak the thoughts that we cannot comprehend, or to say what God might be saying to us. In individual spiritual direction, I felt that Father Abbot almost always spoke wisely, usually not giving specific advice, but always listening closely and speaking with love. In group spiritual direction, not everything that is said to me seems pertinent or moving, but much of what has come up in the past four years has affected me deeply.

In each, there is a radical honesty about ourselves and others. The idea that we are together in God makes the time together sacred, and excessive irony, small talk, or abstraction seems out of place. We have a willingness to see our own sin in

James Kennedy

matters, particularly sin in the sense of personal preoccupation or need to control that separates us from God.

We are prayerful together, that is, willingly open to what God may be saying in our time together, either to us about someone else or to us directly.

Differences Between Individual and Group Direction

Father Abbot is rare and unusual, and a true spiritual director, not easily found. Although he is aware of and involved in our culture to a degree, he is a monk who lives by the Rule of St. Benedict. He has been shaped by a lifetime of living as a monk and his presence reveals that.

I can identify more with my group companions. As I do, they struggle often in their everyday lives and are sometimes lost. They like to avoid suffering—through abstraction, through an eagerness to understand situations, or through lots of words. But, like Father Abbot, with prayer and silence, they genuinely help me see more clearly, although with the group, it is more through my identification with them and through their words to me about what they see and hear.

With Father Abbot, it was mostly one way. I was the center of attention. In group direction, I have a turn at the center, and others have theirs. I am challenged to listen well and carefully and to speak what God might be saying to a person, a challenge I still find daunting and humbling.

In group spiritual direction, the long silences cause our words to stand out and encourage us to be honest with ourselves and God. Abstraction or irony seems profane when the silence allows the words to spill out and linger so long in the mind of the group.

In individual spiritual direction, Father Abbot's words are direct, loving, from God, and encourage me to speak in kind. It is not the silence that brings forth the deeper matters in me but his presence.

Group spiritual direction teaches me patience—occasionally others in the group may be annoying to me because they talk too long, seem to be avoiding an issue, or seem to be avoiding listening to God. I learn to be more patient. I consider what I might say that might be helpful to that person, to me, and to the group. I hold what I hear in silence and ask God how I might respond.

Although Father Abbot never directed me to do this or that, I was willing to submit to his suggestions and ideas, however gently they were presented, because he became authoritative for me by his presence and the way he lived.

Conclusion

It is tempting to write that all is well now, that I live peacefully and surely in everything that I do. Perhaps that is true more often than it used to be, and I suspect that it is. But I know that I can do too much evaluating and judging of my life and my closeness to God, so that my life in God becomes just another accomplishment. It is better that I not think about this. It is better that I take

James Kennedy

to heart the words in this poem written by a friend after we hiked
to a granite outcropping on the Appalachian Ridge overlooking
Holy Cross Monastery at Snicker's Gap, Virginia:

> *Sharp-shinned and red-tailed, they*
> *muscle their way into wind,*
> *once there, glide a thousand*
> *miles to Georgia savannahs,*
> *where they winter, as always,*
> *while below,*
> *on an Appalachian ridge,*
> *a Confederate soldier runs*
> *from battle, dazed and bloody,*
> *stumbles through rocks and thicket*
> *to the top of the ridge, then slumps*
> *like a fallen scarecrow,*
> *and sees black shooting stars*
> *against the white sky.*

It seems to fit, at least symbolically, what has been happening to me in the past six years of spiritual direction—a returning
to a place from my childhood, my participation in and awareness
of a tradition that has been around for more than a thousand
years, and my surrender of willfulness and violence so that I can
see things differently.

II.

================

Group Spiritual Direction Within Communities of Worship

For many reasons, offering group spiritual direction for people within communities of worship makes good sense. Practically speaking, the people who come there often come on a regular basis and are committed to the community for the long haul. This offers the possibility of continuity in groups. The fact that people know that other group members all belong to the same faith community may establish a trust level in groups early on. And since people have been exposed to a common language through worship services, initially there may be fewer communication problems than one might find in groups where members come from diverse settings.

There are, however, drawbacks to offering group spiritual direction within a worship community. I cite these not to discourage you from attempting this, but only to raise your awareness of difficulties others have encountered so that you may take these into account as you pray about the rightness of offering group spiritual direction in your community of worship.

Most people are used to signing up for whatever programs they want in their churches or synagogues. They are not used to a screening process. Yet, not everyone who may do well in other groups is right for group spiritual direction. You should decide ahead of time who will make and convey decisions about acceptance into groups or dismissal from groups, should that become necessary.

You may want to start with a pilot group, where you can test the rightness of the process for your setting. In this case, you might explain the process to those who lead other groups and to committee heads and ask them to suggest people who may be right. People in this pilot group may later prove to be excellent facilitators for other groups. In fact, they may be more effective than people you might naturally ask to be facilitators, such as leaders of other kinds of groups and spiritual directors. People who are not ordinarily seen in leadership or authority roles may more easily hold the entire group accountable for the process they are in together. Using people not generally well known in your worship settings may also curb the tendency for people to sign up for more popular personalities. Usually, however, while you might list facilitators, you would not give people the option of choosing their facilitators, which should be done by the coordinator.

If you are offering group spiritual direction to the worshiping community at large, anything you can do to help people "self-select" appropriately will serve you well in the long run. For example, you might list group spiritual direction along with all the other programs available to this community, being sure to highlight the uniqueness of each program. You might also talk about it at an adult education forum. If you have had a pilot group, members of that group might share their experience with those interested.

People may be reluctant to participate in group spiritual direction in their own worship setting because they are concerned about issues of confidentiality. It is important to say upfront and frequently that what is shared in the group will not be shared outside the group with anyone, including the designated spiritual leader of the community, such as rector or rabbi, or other facilitators. It also is important to assure people that what they have shared in the group will not be brought up for discussion with them outside the group time by any group member without their permission.

Once people are in groups, they may find that they took too much for granted about what they held in common. They may find that they have been using the same words with different meanings. They also may find that their personal spiritualities—who God is for them, how they honor their relationships with God—are very different. Once these differences become apparent, some may be very reticent to share their spiritual hearts with the group lest they be found wanting. They may unconsciously try to subvert the group's intention by raising common issues like the merits of the last sermon they heard or the talents of the new associate. Patience and prayer, coupled with a consistent calling back of the group to its reason for being together, can best serve a facilitator when issues such as these arise.

As implied at the beginning of this essay, none of the potential drawbacks described should deter you from prayerfully considering the invitation to offer group spiritual direction in your own or another worshiping community. They simply invite your vigilance. And, I hope, they encourage you to find a prayer partner or a community of other facilitators to accompany you in prayer and discernment as you make yourself available to God's work in you through group spiritual direction.

I've already spoken of some of the immediate advantages of offering group spiritual direction within a community of worship. There are also long-term advantages, especially when group members are members of committees within this community. Often these people bring elements of group spiritual direction into other community gatherings. They may introduce a prayerful silence at the beginning of a meeting and invite people to allow their prayer to permeate their deliberations, returning to silence when it seems they have lost sight of God. They may become prayer support for governing bodies such as vestries, parish councils, and synagogue boards, gathering separately in prayer as these groups do their work. They may become the nucleus of intercessory prayer groups, inviting others to gather regularly to pray for concerns of their worshiping community and the world. Even if none of these happen, I believe that the presence of group spiritual direction will be a blessing for the entire community in subtle ways that may not be discerned for years. Wherever you have people wanting God and wanting to support others in going for God, tremendous energy is unleashed.

Rose Mary Dougherty

In a Parish Setting

Meg Greeley

Every so often I wake up surprised at what I'm doing these days—coordinating prayer ministries at an Episcopal church, facilitating spiritual direction groups in several parish settings, and heading into training as a spiritual director. Ten years ago anyone who knew me would never have predicted the sharp turn I took out of academics into prayer; I certainly wouldn't have foreseen it, although I've been an Episcopalian all my life. (I did spend about three years attending a UCC church, but that was more than offset long ago by my time in an Episcopal girls' boarding school—morning prayer every day and evening chapel services ensured that there are hymns and canticles I couldn't forget even if I tried.) In any case, although I anticipated going to graduate school when the last of my four children left for college, I find myself now in a very different place.

I first encountered group spiritual direction in my own church. Contemplative prayer was the door I came in, and that

65

led to a ministry of intercession. These prayer ministries have grown from a prayer chain and Sunday morning prayer teams to include a wide range of prayer environments: people who pray on-site for important meetings; permanent "I-teams" (intercessory teams) who pray for all our clergy and other pastoral staff members; temporary I-teams that form and dissolve around programs or special needs; "Nightwatch" intercessors who pray through the night for the gravely ill; "Candlelighters" who pray long-term for people who don't know Jesus; a centering prayer group; and several other groups. The blending of contemplative and intercessory prayer that is present in group spiritual direction is present as well in our prayer ministries. We are used to silence and used to praying for others, so group spiritual direction has never really felt unfamiliar.

I was in a group for about six months and then had the opportunity to attend Shalem's four-day workshop in Denver. At the time, I wasn't even considering facilitating a group—I was just fascinated by the process of the groups and was there to learn more about how they worked. Shortly after the workshop, my rector asked me to work with several parishioners who were in the discernment process for ordination, and that led to an expanded program of group spiritual direction at the church.

The discernment process actually began before I appeared on the scene. One group was in place, because the rector (in response to requests for help in how to listen to God) felt that group spiritual direction (as opposed to one-to-one direction) was where God was taking us. Thus discernment was more about waiting for God to reveal *who* was to develop a program of group spiritual direction rather than *if* we would have group spiritual direction. When I look back, I can see that our church was very ready for this; we had a fair amount of education about prayer and were certainly beginning to grow as people of prayer. I thus consider it very much of God, which isn't to say it didn't take a good deal of work to get going, but as we prayed through it all, everything happened comparatively easily.

My greatest concern personally was that I, a contemplative soccer mom, was in charge instead of a spiritual director, priest, or deacon. I say this to encourage others without a great deal of formal training; obviously some knowledge is needed to work with these groups, but gigantic credentials are not necessarily required. I would hate to see the development of groups in small, out-of-the-way churches diminished by the perceived need for highly trained leadership. The fact remains, though, that my greatest anxiety was that I couldn't do this—which of course put me exactly where I belonged, having to trust in God to make it all work! And God did indeed make it work.

In 1999–2000, we had five groups at my church, and this year we have four (the same number of people, but reconfigured). I'm employed at a UCC church, as a financial secretary, and there are two groups in place there now, with another in the works. (How the financial secretary wound up starting spiritual direction groups continues to mystify us.) I also have trained facilitators and participants at three small Episcopal parishes in the Colorado mountains. Obviously the biggest difference from the Shalem model is that these are parishes whose members see each other frequently in other parish settings, whereas Shalem group members may see each other only once a month. This distinction has a number of ramifications and has resulted in some changes to advertising, selection, and configuring of groups.

I know that contemplative prayer is sometimes considered a fairly arcane activity and thus not for everyone, but if I have learned anything from working with spiritual direction groups, it's that God speaks very powerfully in silence to just about anyone. With this in mind, I'm very careful at church to make clear that these groups are open to all parishioners. Of course, this is ultimately self-selecting, since someone who is not interested in prayer in the first place probably won't inquire; nevertheless, I feel strongly that prayer is not a contest and that anyone who is open to God's working in his or her life and heart should have the opportunity to be in a spiritual direction group. Over and over again, I've seen God move powerfully in the most chatterbox-y of people. It's as though God takes advantage immediately of the smallest amount of silence to speak to them in a most extraordinary way. I won't soon forget the spontaneous psalm God spoke through a usually talkative friend after she'd spent twenty minutes in silence. It was an astonishing gift to the whole group and reminded me once again that this is not about us but about God.

In advertising group spiritual direction, I first run an article for two consecutive months in the church newsletter. This article, which I use every year with very little change, was difficult to write; group spiritual direction is hard to explain even when you have lots of space, to say nothing of when you have only half a page. I quote part of it here, in case it might be useful.

There have been several spiritual direction groups meeting at our parish for a couple of years now, and, since the current groups are ending their period of commitment, it's a good time to invite others who are interested in this process to join us.

Group spiritual direction is difficult to explain without making it seem more complicated than it really is, so maybe it's better to start with what it is not. It is not a prayer group, although prayer is the key element of the process; it's not a sharing group, although sharing is certainly a large part of it; it is not a support group, although spiritual direction is nothing if not supportive; and it is not a place for problem solving, although problems and issues may later be resolved through what happens in this setting.

The defining element of group spiritual direction is intercessory prayer, as all members hold one another in prayer through the meeting, listening to God *with* and *for* each other. The Holy Spirit is thus the real director, and both sharing and responses have their source in God rather than in personal agendas or concerns.

There is lots of silence between periods of talking, and a great deal takes place in this silence. Because of the prayerfulness, spiritual direction groups are a wonderfully safe place and a unique form of spiritual community. Groups of 3–5 people meet

monthly, and this process is not intended to replace
our other small groups.

The second advertising piece is Shalem's video, which I show
during the Sunday education hour for two or three Sundays for
anyone who's interested in knowing more. Questions can be
asked at that time, and the video remains the best way possible
to introduce group spiritual direction. Selection is thus minimal.
People express an interest, and I also invite specific people, who
have come up in my prayer, to pray themselves about being in a
group. (I do this for my church, where I know just about everyone; presumably I would have the sense not to invite someone to
participate for whom group spiritual direction would be inap-
propriate at the time.)

I've thought about what I would do if someone wanted to
participate whom I honestly felt wouldn't benefit from this. I
think the major factor that might make someone not a candidate
would be their seeking solutions to specific personal problems—
seeing the group as a potential form of therapy. In that case, I
would send them to the rector (who oversees this program) for an
appropriate referral.

Configuring the groups, who to place with whom, was one
of the biggest challenges the first few years, but that has been
mitigated by the fact that most groups are choosing to stay
together. At Shalem, groups meet on specified evenings, and participants have to work their schedules around that. That's not
how we do it in our parish, as work and family schedules have to
be considered, along with existing relationships. I first prayed

about it in a general way, asking God to help me figure this out, and then got down to work, putting each name on a file card, praying over all of them, then trying to arrange them. It was frustrating, as every time I thought I had it right, I'd see another snag, sometimes a function of scheduling, sometimes of relationships. Finally, in desperation, I took the cards downstairs and prayed Saint Ignatius's *Anima Christi* prayer for each person by name. (This is not a short prayer, and you can be sure that I now have it memorized—I remember thinking at the time that it was fortunate none of my children were home or they really would think their mother had lost it, praying over a stack of file cards.) As always, God was faithful, and the whole thing fell into place almost immediately.

Between the two local churches (the one where I worship and the one where I'm employed), there are six or seven groups, and clearly I can't facilitate all of them. Involving others as facilitators has worked easily, because the programs grew slowly. People who understand and are committed to the process stand out as potential facilitators. First of all, I've tried to select them very prayerfully, and second, I've tried to keep in close touch with them about how their groups are going and to help them with any issues that arise. The rector at our church attended Shalem's workshop as well, and she's a help, also.

The facilitator piece was more complicated at the three churches in the mountains, even though one of them had a facilitator who had attended the Shalem workshop and also several people experienced in contemplative prayer. They and people from the two other churches met with me on a Saturday, and I showed the Shalem video and presented a 30-minute teaching on additional aspects of group spiritual direction. The three groups then met in a large room, and I facilitated them simultaneously. I don't think I'd do it quite this way again; it was hard to keep track, and when people were confused they didn't tell me. Possibly sheets of paper with the sequence spelled out for each group would have helped.

In May 1999, I went to Virginia for a Shalem workshop about mentoring new facilitators. Since I'd been doing this for several years without a mentor, this gathering of people who were much more experienced than I was extremely helpful, and I received a lot of support from them at that time. It also highlighted for me the importance of supporting the facilitators I've trained and not leaving them on their own. I know that our situation isn't ideal, and more training for facilitators would indeed be wonderful. Since that can't happen easily, I was grateful to have the chance to talk about how to mentor widely scattered facilitators. I try not to let the process be compromised or diluted.

There are three additional aspects to spiritual direction groups that came up out of a lot of prayer about how the groups function in a parish. I'd had a sense, ever since I started out as a group member, that this process is really important, going well beyond the stated functions of spiritual direction. Group spiritual direction has the potential to change churches at a deep level by altering how the people in them relate to each other.

First, the groups appear to me to model clearly, at the smallest and most intimate level, the way churches should operate. They incorporate a number of things visible in the early church as described in the Book of Acts—the centrality and presence of God, the reciprocal and shared prayer, the equality of all in the sight of God. Everything moves through the context of prayer and the central presence of Jesus; the intentional intercessory prayer and listening to God that we do in group spiritual direction are a very visible example of how we might operate all the time, in every arena of the church.

The prayer ministries at our church follow this model, and I think that our participation in spiritual direction groups had a great deal to do with these ministries blossoming as they did. I felt from the beginning that our prayer community was not about "standing in the gap on behalf of the land" (Ezek 22:30)—all facing the same direction—but about a circle of intercessors whose prayer, no matter for whom, is reciprocal and shared. Despite the appearance of structure, we are very much a community that intentionally prays together and whose activities, programs, and relationships are supported by a subtext of prayer. I couldn't have articulated this until recently, but it's clear now that the group spiritual direction process has had a strong impact on the structure of our prayer community. We're learning that prayer is not optional, in our work or in our friendships, and that the Holy Spirit is our director all the time, not just in the groups. From what I've seen so far, the skills people learn in the groups and the deep changes that take place in the participants can significantly affect how a church functions.

A second element of the groups is about relationships that glorify God, about allowing God to be in charge of all our relationships, and the only way to do that is in a context of ceaseless prayer (1 Thess 5:17). In this way, we allow God to write our relationships instead of writing themselves from our own agendas. We often freeze relationships where they start out instead of allowing God to continually rewrite them. In the groups, we can allow God to work and pray through us to script multiple and constantly changing relationships that can truly glorify God. One group member commented last week that spiritual direction groups have a much deeper level of trust than the traditional "prayer and share" gatherings, and the relationships have a corresponding depth as well. She indicated that she never left feeling unheard or diminished.

One of my favorite things about the groups is seeing people who don't necessarily like each other relate entirely differently in an environment of prayer. We learn in the groups how to hold someone in prayer while we interact with them, and conversations informed by prayer can be significantly transformed as we allow the Holy Spirit to work. It's wonderful to get to pray for someone while listening to them, and that can quickly change how we see others, as we look at them from God's perspective. When enough people in a community can do this, there is an atmosphere of prayer that God uses to work powerfully in our relationships.

A third characteristic of these groups, which I've recently noticed and love, is their living out of 2 Corinthians 1:3–4: "Praise be to the God and Father of our Lord Jesus Christ, the father of compassion and the God of all comfort, who comforts us in all our trouble *so that* we can comfort those in any trouble with the comfort we ourselves have received from God" (italics mine). God's compassion comes to each of us in the spiritual direction group process, both through prayer and also through the sharing and response dialogue. Because we are intentionally listening to God in the silence, God can more easily speak compassion through us, and as recipients of that compassion, we can then offer it to others in our church and other communities. A church that has a number of people participating in these groups can have a depth of compassion that is different from compassion as understood by the world. The compassion that is a gift from God is not about being "nice" or "sympathetic"—rather it's about passion, a depth of feeling, and a commitment to prayer and action. The groups are a place (though certainly not the only one) where we can receive the powerful compassion that is from God, not generated by our emotions. Churches that receive this gift can be changed in their responses to all sorts of challenges, and they can then go out to change the world, "comfort[ing] others with the compassion [they] have received from God."

One thing I can be sure of is that we're not through learning how spiritual direction groups operate in and have an impact on local parishes. I find it tremendously exciting to see God's continued working in all of the parish groups that I know about—and I know God is doing the same thing in all sorts of other places. In the midst of the tangle of everyday life and in spite of the significant suffering that we see all around us, these groups provide a unique environment in which we can encounter Jesus. And that makes them a priceless gift to all of us, to our parishes, and to our wider communities.

Raising Holy Sparks

Ann Kline

The Jewish sages teach that every aspect of creation is filled with a hidden, divine light waiting to be revealed and reunited into a whole. The aim of every Jew, according to these sages, is to raise these "holy sparks" of divinity and complete the creation of the world. As scholar David Ariel explains, "By raising the sparks, by recognizing the divine nature of the world [and each other] and finding the sparks everywhere they are hidden, we bring about repair of the world."

This *tikkun olam*—repair of the world—is the essence of what spiritual direction means for me. Through spiritual direction, we pay attention to where those sparks may be found within us, and encourage each other to bring those hidden sparks into the openness of our collective awareness. It is this awareness that can transform our actions into service, freeing us to fulfill our roles as co-creators with God. So, when the opportunity to start a spiritual direction group in a synagogue found me, how could I say No?

I was crazy to say Yes, however. I had only become involved with group spiritual direction the year before. I had just begun to facilitate my first group. What did I know about the process and starting groups? For that matter, I had only just begun to take my own Judaism more seriously. What did I know about being Jewish? But my experience as a Jew involved in prayer and direction with Christians had made me sensitive to the issues facing interfaith seekers. I can still vividly recall my anxiety the first time I walked into a Shalem workshop. Would they try to convert me? Was I being disloyal to my own tradition? How would I feel if they used language like *incarnation, resurrection, prayerfulness?* Would it sound self-conscious if I used words from my tradition: *devekut* (cleaving, union with God), *teshuvah* (return or renewal, return to God's ways), *kavanah* (a focused intention brought to prayer)? Could I even pronounce the Hebrew?

All of those issues faded like mist in the reality of what I experienced. But cultural differences can loom like dragons, discouraging people from following certain paths that could be of enormous benefit in their spiritual journeys. As much as I did not want to encourage those (to me, illusory) barriers, I wanted to share what I was learning with other Jews. I wanted to bring what I was learning "home."

I called this project "Raising Holy Sparks." I needed a name for the group, because awareness of spiritual direction in Judaism—at this writing—is still in its nascent stage. While there are Jewish spiritual support groups of various kinds, a disciplined approach to spiritual examination, with a basis in intercessory prayer, is quite novel. I needed to tie group spiritual direction into something with a traditional foundation to reassure people that this was "Jewish."

I had no idea what to expect. Would anyone sign up? Would I know what to do if they did? My ignorance of the process and the congregation was actually a blessing. I had no choice but to put the whole endeavor in God's hands; I certainly had no idea what I was doing. I made up my mind that, as God had found me with this project, I would trust to God's intention (even if it were to put me in my place through utter disaster).

Relinquishment was made even easier because I knew I had the support of Shalem behind me. Concurrent with the synagogue group, I would be facilitating a group at Shalem. I'd have the opportunity to bring issues and concerns to my peer group sessions at Shalem, where other facilitators would join me in prayer. Knowing that I would have that prayer and support gave me more confidence to proceed. But I was still nervous. It was going to be me and that group—if there were one—alone in a great big synagogue one night a month. Would God bother to show up?

The selection process for participants reflected the "not my will but Thine" approach to this group. With permission, I modified Shalem's brochure to describe the process in ways I hoped would be more understandable to a Jewish audience, and I set out copies in the synagogue. (The text of the announcement I used can be found in the Appendix at the end of this essay.) The group was listed as a course offering in the fall adult education program. People interested in the group were told they first had to contact me. The group was limited to five people. While I think four is the ideal size for a group, I was prepared to take on more in anticipation of someone dropping out.

I did not prepare a set of questions to ask people, although I had an idea of what I wanted to learn from, and say to, each of them. I wanted to know what they were looking for and what appealed to them about the offering. I was as interested in hearing how they spoke about these things as I was in the particular responses. How tentative were they? How clear? What language did they use? What aspects did they choose to emphasize? The more I knew about them, the better able I would be to explain the process in ways that addressed their particular concerns and interests. For my part, I wanted to stress the commitment necessary to sustain the process—that this was not a casual support group.

Six people contacted me. Each conversation was unique as I tried to understand the different voices calling people to this offering. While I had reservations about two of the callers—one asked whether she would have the option of not sharing, and one asked (hopefully) whether I was screening people based on Jewish knowledge—I let the description of the group promote self-selection. I stressed those aspects of the process that addressed each person's concerns so that they would have as clear an idea as I could provide about what would be expected.

I encouraged everyone to come the first night, explaining that commitments would not be expected until after the introductory meeting. Coward that I am, I could not tell anyone "No," feeling inadequate to determine whose calling was legitimate or what that calling might be. I also believed that, because the idea of spiritual direction is so novel within Judaism, people should have an opportunity to get a better sense of the process before they committed to the group.

Five people showed up the first night (self-selection had already worked for the one who wanted to be with a group of knowledgeable Jews, which would have counted me out). As I sat with sweaty palms watching the people gradually fill up the circle of chairs I had made in the school classroom, I kept repeating to myself, *This is Your work, not mine.* I did not have a clue what I was going to say to these people. I was so happy there was a videotape to use; a whole forty-five minutes when I would not have to speak! Shalem has developed an excellent video describing the group spiritual direction process. My only concern in using it was that prominent throughout much of the tape is a large cross in the background. How would these Jewish seekers respond to that?

I could easily imagine that after that night no one would want to continue. I certainly would have been dismayed to walk into the sterile classroom we had been assigned, expected to find spiritual awakening on hard, wooden seats, under glaring fluorescent lights. I imagined that these seekers might ask, "What do you mean we sit in silence?" (Nothing in a synagogue is silent, and even the parts of the service that are not spoken aloud are filled with prescribed words and prayers.) "What do you mean share what is calling my attention in my life; I live a very quiet, ordinary life. What are you going to teach me? What am I going to get out of this? Is this Jewish?"

That sense of "Jewishness"—which I translate as groundedness in tradition—was critical to the group. I called the group's attention to Jewish *midrash* (a particular kind of rabbinic interpretation of the Bible) that tells how, at Sinai, God spoke to each of the Israelites in their own voice. What we do in spiritual direction is to listen to how God speaks to us in our own voices—the details of our daily lives and loves and challenges.

I think that first night can be summed up in one of the participants' comments at the end of the evening: "This is the first time that I have spoken to other Jews about how I feel about God." (This came from a woman in her fifties, very active in the synagogue.) Or perhaps in one woman's revelation that watching a soap bubble had been a moment of intimacy with God, and her recognition of what it meant to claim that. Each participant in the room that evening described in some way a shared longing for more intimacy with the divine. Realizing that they could possibly achieve that through sharing their own life experiences was exciting and a little frightening. It was a moment of revelation for me to realize how much it meant to be present with them, part of an unfolding awareness of possibility. I need not have worried about God showing up; God gathered us in a firm embrace and was not about to let us loose.

81

All five decided to continue. I went home that first night overwhelmed by God's generosity. That this group was going to happen felt as much a miracle to me as the parting of the Red Sea, and I was going to get to witness it. Even more of a miracle, the rabbi offered to donate his office for our meetings—it made a big difference to pray together on comfortable chairs in a quiet, carpeted room where we could dim the lights.

Silence soon became a major issue for the group. After two meetings, one woman (I will call her Sarah) decided she could no longer continue because the silence made her uncomfortable. As a woman living alone, Sarah felt she had enough "silence" in her life. And she did not feel that she was offering much to the group (a way, I believe, of saying that the group was not giving her what she was looking for at the time). It was hard for the group to let her go, and it tried to reassure her that she was valued. But we needed to trust her own discernment. We realized that it would be kinder to let her go with grace than to try to hold her there.

After the first meeting without her, we did not continue to pray for her as a group after she left (although I believe others continued to pray for her individually). I continued to pray for her on my own for awhile, as I struggled with questions. I wondered if there was more I should have done to open the way for her, or if there was something to learn about her need that would have made a difference for her.

I regret not having spent some time with Sarah after the meeting where she made her announcement. At the time,

I felt I needed to respect her decision and not seem to "pressure" her. I thought God had asked a very specific thing of me and I needed to stick to the "one path," my commitment to the group and to the process, and not let other concerns or interests become fuel for distractions. Now, I am not so sure. (I learned later that Sarah had continued to think about the group throughout the year, even remembering when the last meeting was to be so that she could send her regards. I heard, after I was no longer facilitator, that she eventually rejoined the group.)

The experience with Sarah opened the way for others in the group to raise their own discomfort with the silence. Some people did not understand the purpose of silence, particularly during the time of sharing and response. What were they supposed to think about during that time? Some people had hoped to learn more about meditation and wanted me to tell them about techniques they could use. As we worked through the questions, I realized how difficult it can be to convey what it means to be present to God, and to do so for one another. And I felt drawn into the role of "teacher"—not a comfortable role for me—trying to connect these issues to Jewish teaching.

The group asked me to lead it through a guided meditation, which I did at the next meeting. Using a significant Jewish prayer, the *Shema* (Hear, O Israel, the Lord Our God, the Lord Is One), I tried to guide the meditation toward those aspects of the prayer that are about our interconnectedness and our shared role in living out of God's love for us.

Something seemed to "open" for the group after that meditation, although I do not credit anything I said. I think any meditation, led by anyone, would have worked as long as every person in the group felt directed toward a common purpose. I felt, and others commented on this as well, that some new level of "bonding" had occurred and that the group was much more aware of being there for the benefit of each other rather than as individuals there primarily for themselves.

At the conclusion of that meeting I invited someone else to lead the silence the next time. I opened it up to the volunteer (Mark), someone familiar with spiritual retreats, to use the time as he felt appropriate but did not hold him to what I had been doing—sharing a reading.

At the next meeting, Mark led us in a wordless Jewish chant, called a *niggun*. The *niggun* served a similar purpose to a shared reading, directing our attention to a place beyond words where we could just be held together in God. I was afraid that the chanting might intimidate some people not comfortable with singing (like myself) or that it would seem more like a performance than an opportunity for reflection. I need not have worried. One person said that, rather than being intimidating, the beauty of one person's singing gave her courage to sing herself (although not very loudly). And people found that the *niggun* had a meditative effect, giving them new perspective on what they had wanted to share that evening.

If anything, people were more interested in sharing their response or reflections on the *niggun* than they were in what they were experiencing in their daily lives. I was concerned that the chanting could get in the way of our reason for being together, but people responded so strongly to it that I invited Mark to lead us in a *niggun* at the next meeting, after which I spent more time directing people in reflection on their prayer for the group and the world. Again, there was an atmosphere of prayerfulness that hadn't been there in the earlier meetings and that all noticed.

I did not continue with the shared chanting after the second time. While I personally loved starting our time together with a chant, I realized that the true gift of the *niggun* was in bringing us together toward a common purpose. Instead of asking for someone else to facilitate in opening prayer, I went back to the original format of a shared reading to help ground people in that part of the process.

I took greater care after the experience with the *niggun* in the selection of my readings for the group, having more of a sense of what the group might be open to hear and wanting to promote the sense of intercessory prayer. I had a greater appreciation for the need to spend part of the shared silence for some guided meditation toward how the group was praying for each other and the world.

In addition to the issue of silence, the group challenged me to be more active in the role of facilitator than I had been in other groups. At various times people needed to be drawn out in their sharing, struggling to put into words what they had never expressed before, or in some instances struggling to understand how to present what they were experiencing. I learned much from the group about what some people face in trying to claim their spirituality and in trusting God's love working in their lives. I became very aware of the facilitator's vital function of modeling the process, constantly bringing people's focus back to how God might be reflected in their experiences.

More than anything else, I learned to trust God as God worked in the group. If something presented itself as an issue, time and prayer soon showed that the issue either resolved itself or the group was more than able to address it without me. After the first few meetings, and very few instances when I had to redirect responses away from problem solving, the members seemed to settle into a sense of how to be with each other that needed very little more from me than a nudge here and there to have more confidence in what they had to share. I felt freed to more fully participate in the responses.

Time spent with this group felt very graced, for me personally and for the group. After one meeting, someone came up and thanked me for "the way I was with the group." I believe he was commenting on a sense of shared experience. To him, I was not an "other" in the group, a referee calling time, but a full participant even though I did not share my personal journey. I felt that maybe I was doing something right.

Even more, I appreciated how people summarized their experience of the group process. Members remarked how the group had given them greater confidence in their spiritual aspirations, a greater trust that God was actually speaking to them. They expressed a greater willingness to listen. There were no breakthroughs, no instances of great insight, revelation, or conversion. There was, however, in the words of the group, a sense of ease and affirmation that came from being able to express the deepest desires of their hearts with other people who understood.

They spoke of how their experience with the group had made them more aware of God. They looked at their lives a little differently, reflecting them through the lens of "Where is God in this?" They listened to Torah (the Bible) differently, relating to the stories more personally because of their experience in listening to the Torah of their own lives. They even learned to love the silence. (Some mothers remarked they were able to listen to their children better, resisting the pull to intervene as much as they might have before the group experience.)

I was gratified when the group decided to continue. One person was reluctant to do so because I wouldn't be the facilitator. It was tempting to be seduced by the wonderful things people said into believing that perhaps they still needed me. After all, I was so incredibly wise and sensitive and insightful. But if there was real value in what they were doing, if God was truly at work in this group, they would never have the chance to fully experience that as long as they confused what was happening with me (or any guide). I, too, needed the lesson in humility in letting them go. This was God's group, not mine.

Their feedback on my contribution as a facilitator, however, was gratifying. I often wonder if the role of facilitator is no more than a glorified timekeeper. I constantly ask myself what I add to (or detract from) the process, how it would be different if I were not there. Am I doing too much and encouraging the group to rely on me more than each other? Am I doing too little and not using the opportunity I have to help people understand how to use the process to probe a little deeper, see a little more expansively, hear a little more clearly, trust God a little more willingly?

Concurrent with this group, I was experiencing my first year in individual spiritual direction. I frequently reflected on the differences and similarities between the processes and on how my director was with me compared to how I was with the group. In individual direction, I can listen more to how God is speaking through the chorus that is the many aspects of my own life. In group direction, where individual sharing must be more selective, everyone in the group becomes God's chorus as I hear God speaking through each person's life experiences. Accordingly, the two processes provide different windows on intimacy with God; if individual direction provides more opportunity to focus on God's intimacy with "me," group direction can serve to emphasize God's intimacy with "us."

Among what the processes share, however, is how the simple act of our coming together provides a quiet, constant reminder of the one who is the source of all. One of the most significant gifts I received through my spiritual director was her affirmation of my faithful search for God simply by being with me in it. That realization gave me greater confidence to just "be there" with this group. It was the most important thing I, as a facilitator and as a human being, had to offer.

At the end of our time, we discovered we needed a ritual for saying good-bye. At Shalem, the groups all gather together, arms entwined, for a chant of "Shalom." We, too, gathered in a circle but felt the need for a more traditional Jewish blessing. We chose the prayer that Jewish tradition says should be recited when embarking on a journey. It felt fitting to say a prayer about beginnings, rather than endings. For this group, the journey was still unfolding.

May it be your will, O Lord my God,
to lead us in peace,
to guide our steps in peace,
to save us from any enemy or entrapment along the
way,
to bless the works of our hands
and permit us to find grace, favor, and mercy in
Your eyes
and in the eyes of all who behold us.
Blessed are You, O Lord, who hears prayer.

Appendix:
An Invitation to Group Spiritual Direction

Remove your shoes, for the place where you are standing is holy ground.

—*Exodus* 3:5

Do not fear....I have called you by name. You are mine.

—*Isaiah* 43:1

89

Ann Kline

What does it mean for God to "call us by name"? How can our lives be seen as "holy ground"? How can we use these questions to create spiritual community?

We can become aware. We can open ourselves to an honest exploration of our relationship with God. We can quiet ourselves to hear how God is being reflected in the lives of others. We can join together to raise our holy sparks, the light of the divine within us that, collectively, can heal the world.

What Is Group Spiritual Direction?

Drawing upon other spiritual traditions, group spiritual direction is a process whereby a group of people gather on a regular basis to become more aware of how God is working in their lives. It is a meditative process, in that it is a disciplined approach to spiritual reflection, through the sharing of experiences, reflective listening, silence, and response. It is also meditative in that its "effect" is cumulative. Only by ongoing commitment to the process and to the others in the group can new insight and openness, and community, emerge.

What Does Participation in a Group Entail?

Group spiritual direction requires two things of the participants: (1) members must be willing to open their spiritual journeys for consideration by others; and (2) members must whole-heartedly participate in the group experience by reflective listening and response, attendance and reflection upon the group between meetings. All members should share the desire to grow closer to God and to create a trusting, supportive atmosphere in which to foster that desire in themselves and others.

Groups consist of 3 to 5 people who meet for 2 1/2 hours, once a month, for eight months. A facilitator assists the process so that participants can concentrate on the sharing and response rather than the clock. The facilitator also assists the group in understanding the dynamics of the process and keeping people on track.

Before a group begins, the facilitator will provide people an opportunity to assess whether group spiritual direction is right for them at that time through an introductory presentation. That presentation will include a detailed description of the process and, if possible, a demonstration. The informational meeting also will provide the opportunity to share as a group what prompted each of them to consider group spiritual direction and what each hopes to find through the process.

Once the choice is made to participate, members must commit to attend every meeting (barring unforeseen circumstances). Between meetings, members commit to reflection on their spiritual journeys in whatever manner seems right to them (for example, some people maintain journals) and to holding the group in their hearts and minds in whatever manner seems appropriate (for example, some people say a daily prayer, or daily spend a moment envisioning the group with a sense of well-being).

Ann Kline

How Does the Process Work?

Each meeting begins with a time of silence (about 20 minutes) to allow participants to dedicate themselves to the time ahead. After the silence, the facilitator invites someone to begin sharing when he or she is ready. While the person is sharing (for about 10–15 minutes) the other participants listen in an open and reflective manner without interrupting the speaker. When the speaker is finished, there is a time for silence (about 3 or 4 minutes) that provides the members with the opportunity to go deeper than their reflexive reactions and respond from a more open and attentive place. Members then share the questions or thoughts that arose for them for the speaker during that time (about 10 minutes). There is another period of silence (about 3 minutes) in which members hold the person who has just shared in their hearts and minds. The facilitator then invites someone else to share, and the process of sharing-silence-response-silence is repeated until everyone has presented.

Time (about 10 minutes) is reserved at the end of the meeting to reflect on the quality of the time together, how the process did or did not work for that meeting, how open the group was to each other.

Who Is the Facilitator?

Ann Kline is committed to exploring and developing contemplative spirituality within the context of Judaism. To that end, she has been a participant in and a facilitator of spiritual direction groups at the Shalem Institute for Spiritual Formation in Bethesda, Maryland. She works part-time as an attorney for the U.S. Environmental Protection Agency and spends her other time working as a hospice volunteer, writing fiction, and taking care of Howard, her husband, and Hannah, their dog. Ann will be available outside of meetings to provide whatever assistance and support she can for the participants' spiritual self-discovery through this process.

Spiritual Discernment Groups in a Congregational Setting

Judith Brown Bryan and Trevor Watt

> *For where two or three are gathered in my name, I am there among them.*
>
> —*Matthew 18:20*
>
> *For God alone my soul waits in silence.*
> —*Psalm 62:1*

In a short eighteen-month period, spiritual direction groups have become a vital part of the life of our parish in Buffalo, New York. In hindsight, we recognize the Spirit's leading the church and its leaders:

- The vision of the new senior pastor as he discerned a need in the congregation and his trust and validation of the initiative;

- The synchronicity of Trevor's spiritual journey;

- The endorsement of the church governing body; and

- The commitment of six members of two early groups to be trained as group facilitators.

The constellation of timing and persons seems providential. We begin by briefly tracing the evolution of spiritual direction groups at our church.

Trevor attended a Shalem retreat in 1998, after which he entered personal spiritual direction. That winter, he enrolled in a course on group spiritual direction at a nearby seminary. Course readings included Rose Mary Dougherty's book, *Group Spiritual Direction*, and a viewing of her videotape, as well as a weekly experience of group spiritual direction.

Trevor was deeply moved by the experience of praying and being prayed for by the small group. From this experience, he approached his pastor and proposed to lead a group in his parish. The pastor expressed interest and explored with Trevor a vision of how members of the congregation could be mentored to become facilitators. He suggested that Trevor begin with a presentation and invitation to the elected governing body of the church. By the summer, two groups of board members had participated in seven discernment sessions, meeting every other week over the course of three months.

Six of these participants were invited and agreed to be mentored as they facilitated their new groups. Judith was among this group. During the fall, they met every two weeks.

The first half-hour was given to a discussion of a chapter in Dougherty's book. Each person then took a turn facilitating a group. The time concluded with an extended discussion of leadership, participation, and process. Through Shalem's extension program for facilitating group spiritual direction, Trevor received guidance and mentoring. This was the formal beginning of the church's program in group spiritual direction.

Our church is a 150-year-old, downtown metropolitan church of approximately 1,000 members. It has a venerable history of social action and justice in its community. Progressive in its politics and liberal in its support for freedom of thought, it attracts a well-educated congregation. Thirty-three percent of its members have B.A. degrees or equivalents; 34 percent have a M.A. or Ph.D.; and two-thirds of its members are professionals. It is a cerebral, active congregation whose emphasis is on God at work in community.

Our church has a developing spiritual vocabulary. In a self-study anticipating a new pastorate, "spirituality" did not even appear among a list of twenty items designed to elicit priorities. Biblical and theological expertise was more strongly preferred than spirituality in a new pastor. Our experience with corporate silence was limited; the longest silence in worship lingered about one minute. Nevertheless, the church's mission study task force charged that "we are, above all, called to listen for God's word and to strengthen our understanding of God's purpose." The new pastor is well equipped and committed to helping the church develop skills and a vocabulary to listen more clearly for God's leading. He observes that new and old members are eager to find a forum to explore their faith and relationship with God; they are hungry for spiritual food. One of his early initiatives was to identify a parish associate position for spiritual formation. Hence it is in the context of a Reformed congregation, with a new pastorate committed to spiritual growth and a sanctioned leader for spiritual formation, that spiritual direction groups were introduced.

Once group spiritual direction had been introduced to the church leadership and facilitators had been identified and trained, we looked to establish new groups for the winter–spring season. To promote the groups to the congregation, we planned several approaches.

The most important ingredient in the launching was the senior pastor's active interest and endorsement. In conjunction with the pastor's own initiative of small group ministries, we planned a luncheon meeting after church one Sunday. Announcements were included in the semi-monthly newsletter, and a full-page flyer (Appendix A) was inserted in the Sunday bulletin two weeks prior to the luncheon. Another technique, perhaps the most effective, was a personal letter mailed directly to new members, the caregivers team, parents of middle and senior high students, church officers, the women's and men's groups, Sunday school teachers, and Family Life Committee members. We drafted a letter that called attention to the pastor's support and invited people to come and learn more about group spiritual discernment. Finally, information (Appendix B) and sign-up sheets with the names of facilitators and the schedule for the group were available to the entire congregation on a table with the other church activities over a period of weeks prior to and after the informational gathering.

Approximately fifty members attended the informational luncheon meeting. Trevor introduced the history and purpose of group spiritual direction at our church. Each facilitator introduced him- or herself by summarizing the value and meaning of group spiritual direction in his or her own life and indicated the schedule anticipated for his or her group. It was anticipated that groups would meet six times, approximately every other week during Lent. At the end of the meeting, the attendees were invited to sign up for the time or facilitator of their choice or to turn in their preference sometime in the week. Most of the groups were formed that afternoon. Groups were composed of white, middle-aged men and women, and with a few exceptions, participants had their affiliation with the church and the Reformed tradition in common. Some had rich prayer lives; others longed to deepen theirs.

Although Shalem groups typically meet monthly, we found that, in our urban church setting, we needed to compact the time frame. Partly this was due to the unfamiliarity of spiritual direction groups in the Reformed tradition. Also, quite a few church members were unable to commit themselves to a specific day and time for a whole year, since many had changing work, educational, or social schedules. Because these initial groups were pilot programs, it seemed sensible to experiment with a schedule of meeting six or seven times over a three-month period. Some groups experimented with holding the first few meetings over three successive weeks, followed by monthly gatherings.

Overall, group members attuned quickly to the new style of discernment-direction, and the groups cohered rapidly. We continue to experiment with the schedule, recognizing that the rhythm and frequency of the gatherings are intrinsic to the experience.

Before the first meetings of the individual groups, the facilitators met with Trevor to plan the format. In addition, each facilitator arranged for a meeting place and telephoned her participants to welcome them and provide information about time and place. Some facilitators provided participants with a short piece on prayer or spirituality. From the beginning of the first group, we found that some members asked for material to read between the meetings.

Creating and acknowledging sacred space and time has been helpful in communicating the unique nature of group spiritual direction. Facilitators create ambience by placing the chairs in a circle; a central table holds the candle, chime, or gong, and any other item to create sacred space. Paper and pens are provided for journaling. The gongs have varied from those with Christian symbols to Tibetan bowls and Asian temple bells. Our musicians are ready to experiment in the next sessions with flutes, violins, and other instruments. We find that musical markers to enter and exit silence are preferable to and less intrusive than verbal instructions, however gently delivered. One group used nonverbal hand signals to encourage someone to speak up and to redirect participants who were entering conversation, instead of speaking out of the leading of the Holy Spirit. Another group made a clear transition from social time to sacred time before and after the gatherings by arranging for snacks and conversation to occur in one room and then moving to the church library where sacred space was respected.

At the first meeting, each facilitator opened with a three-minute period of silence, followed by a welcome and introductions, including the participants' interest in group spiritual direction. Confidentiality was stressed as essential to the group's comfort and success.

Each facilitator had been encouraged to make use of ritual to open and close the session (with candle lighting, for example) and to demarcate the periods of silence with a chime or gong. The facilitators provided information to participants about the purpose and format of the session, including brief remarks about the purpose and value of silence. The focal question for the first session, borrowed from Rose Mary Dougherty's *Group Spiritual Direction*, concerned the individual's spiritual journey and the gifts each brought to the group.

The format for the first meeting included a minute of silence for reflection on the question, opportunity for one person to offer a response, another minute for the group to reflect on that response, then time for others to respond to the first response. The process was repeated for each group member who chose to participate. Eight to ten minutes were allowed at the end of the session to process the experience with participants, concluding with another minute of silence and then followed by a closing prayer.

Subsequent sessions followed a similar format: time to check in with each other, entering the silence, posing a question or theme for prayer, reflection, and response, concluding with a time for processing, silence, and verbal prayer. Variations reflected group needs and the Spirit's working in facilitators. One facilitator planned a forgiveness ritual, for example. Another invited participants to bring in quotes or prayers to share.

Sharing spiritual questions, joys, and issues in an atmosphere of trust quickly bonds a group in a sense of intimacy. This proved true not only for those who met for the first time but also for those who had known each other socially. Many participants commented on how shared silence led them in a surprising way to a sense of closeness.

The ending of a group that has experienced this kind of intimate disclosure of self with God and others can bring up anxiety. We believe it is wise to acknowledge and name the associated feelings by the fourth session and to begin preparing for closure.

The sixth and final session was constructed to provide closure for participants and the facilitator. Facilitators selected a variety of ways to do this. For instance, one way was to ask members at the second-to-last meeting to reflect on the God-given spiritual gifts they had received and on those given to fellow participants. These reflections and their variations provided a potent and profound means of closure. One variation was to invite each to name the ways that God delights in every one of us. Another was to reflect positively on a "hidden" talent that they would like to see developed or encouraged in other participants. A third variation encouraged participants to identify what had been going on between God and the individual during the weeks or months together. In addition, each person might be invited to bring a symbol of his or her relationship with God to be placed on the central table and spoken of briefly. In the future, groups may choose to conclude by anointing the hand or forehead of each participant with fragrant oil. A final silence, prayer, and opportunity to process the benefits and challenges of participating in a spiritual direction group complete the session.

Facilitators noted the challenge of listening and facilitating the group process. As one emphasized, "It's scary to be a facilitator!" A variety of concerns challenged them.

All agreed that the first period of silence can feel ominously long, even tense. While most affirmed that silence became a welcome gift for individuals and for the group, a few found that the periods of silence felt contrived and too lengthy. As one participant identified, she has lived alone amidst much silence for eleven years, so silence in a group setting, where she might expect conversation, felt especially lonely for her.

Providing readings about the process was helpful to some groups, and most facilitators found that they needed to review the process of silence-speaking, silence-response at the beginning of each session. Some facilitators tried easing the tension with a word or "Okay" to give participants the permission they seemed to need to begin speaking.

The facilitators found that each group develops its own style, dependent on the personalities of participants and facilitator and the interactions among them. One group may have several highly verbal or enthusiastic members; another may have more reflective and introverted members. It is important to recognize that the "slow starter" is not necessarily withholding but may, in fact, provide a depth of response and sharing when given time. It may take more time to develop a sense of group trust if participants are slower to respond. But one facilitator discovered the unparalleled joy of spending a full hour in silence in the church courtyard, where the group had gathered under a dogwood tree in full bloom.

Facilitators also wondered how "big" or "small" to be within the group, how much of an active presence they needed to be. They were required to do more redirecting, reminding, and refocusing than they had anticipated. Some found it difficult to keep the structure of the process and the time frame without being rigid or authoritarian. Some found that timekeeping and facilitating are easier if shared with a cofacilitator.

In a church setting, it is virtually impossible to screen or exclude anyone who signs up for a group. Therefore, a problem that surfaces will need to be addressed once the group has begun. The facilitators learned that sometimes, if one or two were absent, the facilitator might find it appropriate to participate more actively. Or, if a needy group member were dominating the group's time or persisting in social conversation, the facilitator might need to be more directive. A group member whose responses are appropriate but who interrupts the silence prematurely may need a reminder to wait quietly for the Spirit's prompt or at least for the facilitator's okay.

Group trust is undermined when members speak imperson-
ally or seldom, and several facilitators remarked that participants
needed support to speak out of their own feelings and experience
or out of God-given wisdom. For example, some participants, who
felt more comfortable beginning a sentence with "Everyone" or
"Once my friend had that happen" needed encouragement to
speak more directly to what had been said and to speak out of their
own listening.

One facilitator found that she needed to set aside for a time
the prescribed process and to help the group develop a vocabulary out of which to name God's leading in their lives. She listened for threads in the dialogue and summarized them: "What
I hear God saying here…" and then framed a new question to
take into silence. One of her participants had hoped that the
process would include even more teaching than it had, although
she acknowledged that "we learn from shared stories and experience" as well as from the facilitator. By the group's end, members had begun to take more responsibility for the group's work
and encouraged each other's participation.

For the facilitators, listening at three levels—for content, for
the Spirit's leading of the individual, and for the Spirit's leading
of the group—was a new skill. They had to learn to be a vehicle for
the Holy Spirit, rather than a problem solver or group manager.

Facilitators discovered that the time demands of the program exceeded expectations. In addition to the ninety-minute
meetings, they had to prepare for the meeting, set up and recon-
figure the room, have periodic contact with participants around

schedules, meet for mentoring monthly, and discuss their concerns with their mentor in the interim.

In a congregational setting, it is vital to highlight the covenantal nature of spiritual direction groups in order to distinguish them from other types of church gatherings or meetings. When there is a network of relationships, lengthy histories of families and friendships, regular contact, and an easy familiarity, there may be hesitancy about sharing in a congregational setting. Facilitators must make clear to participants the importance of confidentiality, negotiate a covenantal relationship that includes confidentiality, and provide frequent reminders about keeping confidentiality. Group participants *must have confidence* that nothing they talk about during a session will be told outside the group. It is a challenge to describe the nature of these groups to the curious without violating the confidentiality of fellow participants.

Facilitators needed a forum to raise questions, address challenges, give and receive feedback, pray together around unexpected challenges and concerns. Trevor was readily accessible for individual mentoring by phone, at church on Sundays, and in our monthly gatherings. He willingly processed individual and group concerns.

However, it was frustrating that amidst the concrete demands of launching a new program, we were unable, in our monthly meetings, to include time for silence and reflection, to listen as a group for God's leading. Consequently, we agreed to allow twice as much time for group mentoring. We anticipate two-hour meetings monthly; the first hour will be our own

105

facilitators' group spiritual discernment, and the second hour will allow us to address concrete items of scheduling, calendar, and other practical matters.

Scheduling may be an issue in a congregational setting. Vacation plans and erratic work schedules challenge group cohesion. One group found that three consecutive weekly gatherings, followed by three that were scheduled for every other week, quickly created a sense of intimacy. Another group felt six sessions were too short, so this group agreed to resume again in the fall. A third group with a number of retirees, who often vacation during the winter months, found that scheduling during the Lenten season meant there were few meetings when all participants were present. A fourth group met weekly for six weeks. The facilitator of this group wondered if the frequency of their meetings led to the high level of participation that this group experienced.

One of the challenges that remains unresolved is the imbalance of participants in favor of women. Our hope is for a program that is equally inviting and nurturing for men as for women. Despite the wide range of available groups and times, there were many fewer male participants than female. Interestingly, some facilitators noted that the men who did participate were more likely to break the first silence, thereby facilitating the process.

One of the delights for the facilitators was to discover that, somewhere after the first couple of sessions (when the process may have felt awkward), the groups shifted into a more intimate and comfortable rhythm. Silences were often welcomed;

blessings were offered; members brought in prayers and quotes to share with the group. Each of the facilitators felt blessed by the sincere commitment participants made to the process and schedule as well as by the mutual commitment to pray and be held in prayer between sessions. For example, in one group, when a member had to be absent one week, she forwarded a letter to the facilitator reflecting on how she observed God's presence in each participant's life.

As the process became integrated and participants took more and more responsibility for it, facilitators largely became timekeepers. Most important, the facilitators discovered that when they could relax into the Spirit's leading, the group time flowed easily. As one facilitator remarked, "God gives us the strength; we merely implement the process." Another facilitator commented that she had a sense that God was using her as a catalyst, yet the responsibility for each participant was with God and that person.

The time allotted to process the group meeting at the end was important. Even the sessions that had felt most awkward to the facilitator weren't awkward to most of the participants. Facilitators began to feel that God invites each to express his or her unique and God-given individuality in the facilitator role. "How awesome it is," exclaimed one, "that groups can be so different using the same process." The Spirit leads some through words, others through drawing and journaling. Groups can accommodate both the introvert and extrovert.

Another delight that strengthened the facilitators was to learn that there were so many spiritually aware individuals

107

ready to hear God's leading. Christian maturity permits more growing in a group that is not offering advice but holy listening. In this new setting, participants discover new ways of listening and speaking about their faith and beliefs. This can lead to an intimacy that carries over into Sunday and weekday encounters.

Many participants remarked on the sense of peace that they felt during the group sessions. As one member remarked, "We have too little peace in our lives." Another reflected that receiving stories from others is life giving and a reminder that we are, indeed, "wounded healers." A third person expressed wonderment at the Holy Spirit providing words to a prayer that seemed to flow through her. Many commented on the blessing of being known and getting to know fellow church members at a deeper level, after a long social relationship.

Unique to a congregational setting, perhaps, is the revelation that God's leading can be discerned for the congregation as a whole, as well as for the individual. Participants in one group wondered aloud how what they had experienced might apply to the congregational life of the church. They identified that the very silence and sharing that created a sense of support, community, and intimacy and that had deepened their relationship with the holy can inspire the congregation to be the church God calls it to be: life giving, communal, peace focused. They heard that part of God's call to them is to respond to other church members as they had to each other: listening reverently and without judgment, seeking the Spirit's presence in each encounter. They also concluded that just as

God works through the pastor, the people in the pews, and through the strangers who come through the doors of the church each week, God may also work through the people they encounter in their daily lives.

Another group felt that praying with others, much like worship, is strengthening in a way that individual prayer is not. Often personal formation is nurtured best in the group context, where we experience Christ's promise of presence when two or more are gathered in his name. Other participants identified the joy of praying for fellow participants and members of the congregation with a sense of who they were on the inside and also knowing that the others were praying for them. There is a deep sense of grace in being known by another in a new and more intimate way, particularly when there has been a social relationship through church life. All the members of our group have a personal relationship with God, but what is important in groups is that they also have an experience of community and of each other with God.

Listening for God's leading individually and in small groups has implications for the whole body of Christ. At this time, many forms of popular spirituality are being criticized, accurately, for feeding into our cultural, individualistic narcissism. Spiritual direction in a group setting can reveal God's leading for a congregation, as well as for an individual or small group. Out of our experience of spiritual direction groups, a new committee was initiated, the Spiritual Life Committee. Its mission is to awaken, enhance, and nurture the spiritual life of the church members for the work of ministry. Its objectives are to:

- Identify spiritual needs,

- Develop programs that focus on Christian faith and life, and

- Be a resource for existing programs in order to equip our church community for ministry to the wider community.

The continued encouragement and support by the pastorate and lay leadership is essential to our future. We continue to listen for the needs of the congregation and to expect the guidance of the Holy Spirit as we look to nurture the spiritual life of church members. New groups are already forming, and there are plans to mentor an additional group of facilitators this year.

This is a time of renewal at our church, and the presence of spiritual direction groups is part of a new energy and vision. The new pastor, in reflecting on the impact of direction groups, affirms their meaning and significance even in the short period of time since they were introduced. He also lifts up their value in attracting new members and in revitalizing the life of the current congregation. He affirms that the presence of the direction groups already means that we are able to talk with prospective new members about having an organized, regularly scheduled opportunity for people to explore their faith journey.

This is important, because people who are already attending, as well as those joining the church, are here not primarily for social reasons or because of family history but because they are truly searching and seeking. They have questions about life and faith, and if we do not provide a forum and use faith language to talk about what it means to be on a quest, then we will not be able to offer people what they are most deeply seeking. The impact for our outreach is tremendous!

Our pastor suggests that people who gather regularly in direction groups to talk about their personal experience of the Holy Spirit or God in their lives find validation for everything else that they do. Successful churches are not measured in terms of members, giving, worship, or attendance, but are churches that take the religious task seriously. This may be a reaction or response to the era when churches placed more emphasis on the political than on the religious. Spiritual direction groups and a Spiritual Life Committee contribute in a vital way to who we are and what we do.

To have groups that are talking about faith helps the whole congregation come to grips with how we communicate about our inner, private life. Talking about faith is something like talking about money in a church. It is awkward. There is a fear of sounding too zealous, even too "religious." When you have more people participating in such groups, eventually it makes it all right for those who may be holding back, or afraid, or resisting the opportunity to take a look at their own spiritual journey and at how they could nurture their faith experience. These first groups are really the pioneers.

The pastor believes that having the groups benefits the church family because they increase the level of trust and intimacy in a congregation. Morton Kelsey says that sharing faith experience is the last thing people are willing to risk because this exposes us at our most intimate core. To have groups that do this shows that we can trust each other, and this trust filters into the life of the church. As a result, we see an increased level of concern for one another.

Finally, having direction groups, and all that they symbolize, underscores that our lifeline as individuals, and as a church, is the extent to which our life is lived in, with and by the Spirit. That is what makes us different from the United Way or the Rotary. When we open ourselves to the Spirit, we give over control of our situation to God, and then the boards become bolder, lay leaders become more concerned about what God might want or where God is leading.

Spiritual direction groups contribute to an overall emphasis, subtle and direct, upon our spiritual life. They help us discern God in our midst and God's will for us as a congregation.

Appendix A:
Spiritual Discernment Groups Begin

- Do you sense that God is inviting you into a closer relationship?

- Do you yearn for a spiritual community?

- Do you wonder if others have spiritual struggles and spiritual joys?

- Have you wanted to give more attention to your prayer life?

Perhaps a spiritual direction group is for you.

In a spiritual direction group, four to six persons covenant to meet six times for an hour and a half each time. They covenant to sit with each other in prayer, in listening, speaking, and silence. They covenant to look for God moving in their lives. They covenant to pray for each other between meetings.

Do you feel the Spirit nudging?

- You are invited to a brunch, Sunday, January 23, following church. You will learn more and meet group leaders trained by Rev. Dr. Trevor Watt, Parish Associate for Spiritual Formation.

- Group meetings will take place during the day and evening. Choose which works best for your schedule.

Is God calling you in this direction?

Appendix B:
A Spiritual Discernment Group

IS:

- 4–6 people covenanting together to look for God moving in their lives.

- Prayerful listening and prayerful responding to how God is active in our lives.

- Prayerfully discerning how the Holy Spirit is leading in our lives.

- Praying for each other between meetings.

- Becoming a spiritual community that keeps confidentiality and that celebrates each person's unique desire for God.

- Spending time in silence, listening to God, together.

IS NOT:

- Advice giving, problem solving, or group therapy.

GROUPS usually meet every other week for three months.

Prayerfulness
in a Parish Community

Franklin Adkinson

*In [Christ Jesus] you...are built together spiritually
into a dwelling place for God.*

                                        —Ephesians 2:22

Scripture tells us that God's way is often not our way, and that
the path laid out for us can be circuitous and confusing.
Sometimes only in retrospect can sense be made of our journey.
When my own path brought me to the Shalem Institute, and
then to group spiritual direction, I had no vision of where this
was leading apart from feeding my own soul. Eight years later, I
can look back and wonder whether God was in part preparing
me to assume a leadership role during a difficult transition
period for my local parish.

    First came a heightened personal awareness of the reality
and vitality of a praying Spirit at the center of my being. My

practice of group spiritual direction at Shalem was the essential beginning of this transformation and remains the principal source of its grounding. What I didn't know then was that God would ask me to model, for the benefit of my parish congregation, the prayerfulness, the spaciousness for God, and the yielding to the will of the Spirit that I had begun to experience in spiritual direction.

When our children were young, my wife and I settled on the local Episcopal church in our neighborhood to provide a spiritual home for our family. We had been seekers in a variety of churches in the past but felt that stability was important for our children's religious education. We were attracted to this church by its excellent Anglican music and choirs, by the warm piety of its clergy, and, as is common, by friends who introduced us to the congregation. Our church community was conservative and traditional in its liturgy, largely centered in its Sunday worship and wonderful church music, pastorally oriented, and slowly declining in its membership, which was aging rapidly. Our children grew up there and sang in the choir, we taught Sunday school and supported the music events, and eventually I was elected to the vestry.

The rector and I became good friends for unexplained reasons; he inadvertently became a spiritual teacher to me over the years through his sometimes inspired preaching and the example of a life faithfully lived. His failing health led to an early retirement, and knowing this was coming, he asked me to accept his nomination to be senior warden. When a long-term rector retires in the Episcopal church, the senior warden and vestry are often called upon to preside over a year's preparation for the rector's retirement, followed by an interim process that includes self-study and discernment for the entire congregation, the formation of a search committee for a new rector, the selection of interim priests, and eventually inviting a new rector to lead the congregation. After a weekend retreat of prayer and reflection, I decided to accept this call to leadership. I prayed that God would find a way for me to bring a prayerful spirit to the process.

During the preceding five years, the Shalem Institute had come to be an important spiritual home for me. I found there a wellspring of contemplative riches and role models for lives immersed in prayer and presence. A painfully slow conversion from a life of professional striving and never-enough achievements was beginning to take shape, nurtured in large part by my ongoing commitment to group spiritual direction at Shalem. There each month I was graced with the experience of learning how to be present to God on behalf of the souls of others, as they discerned God's presence and will in their lives. There I learned to listen more and speak less. There I was taught by example and by practice how to harness my own willfulness in hopes of hearing the call of the Spirit. There I sometimes was given the peace and assurance that comes only from yielding to the Holy One. There I grew to experience my life as interwoven with the lives of others and I began to understand the reality of the communion of saints. Shouldn't this prayerfulness be at the heart of the discerning process for an avowedly spiritual community like my parish church? I felt called to make it so and believed that it would be easier to accomplish in a church community than in a secular workplace.

In my fifteen years of parish life, I don't recall prayer being a sincere part of any vestry or committee meetings within the church. Other than the perfunctory grace before meals and an occasional benediction when a priest was present, prayer was relegated to Sunday worship and other ritual occasions. And only clergy "prayed." For most in the congregation, corporate prayer meant to read a prayer from the *Book of Common Prayer*. So, shortly after my election to senior warden, I asked the vestry to appoint a chaplain whose role would be to begin each vestry meeting with a time of prayer and Bible study or meditation. Fortunately, we had a gifted, contemplatively grounded woman who was persuaded to take up this mantle, which she did with sensitivity and graciousness. Silent prayer and centering exercises became a regular part of vestry life, and the tone of our deliberations improved slowly but I believe palpably over time. We became more sensitive to the spiritual nature of our mission and less focused on the church's "business." Our common desires began to outweigh our differences. Our language began to change, as some began to speak openly about "discerning God's plan for our future" rather than just "finding a new rector."

While an increasing majority came to embrace and value the silence, prayer, and scripture reflections with which our meetings began, a few remained uncomfortable or unconvinced. I remember one or two who not-so-passively expressed their objections by routinely arriving fifteen minutes late for vestry meetings. Others acquiesced reluctantly at first but later came to endorse the value of centering our minds and hearts together. A few remained cynical to the end. While this resistance undoubtedly held back our fullest sense of Christian community, it did not defeat our common purpose. Whether prayers were offered for the healing of our differences, only God knows.

Other church committees began to incorporate simple Bible study and prayer to begin any meeting lasting longer than an hour. The vestry had called for this, attempting to honor a new vision of spiritual regeneration for the parish, born out of prayerful consensus in a weekend retreat. So, during our two-and-one-half-year transition period, as we held six all-parish meetings to discuss our process, ventilate our fears, share our hopes, and reflect on our self-study program, we allotted up to twenty minutes for Bible study and prayer, sometimes breaking up into small groups. This was a new experience for most in the congregation, and in general it was well received. I believe it also helped knit us into something closer to the body of Christ about which Paul spoke.

There were dissenters, however, and some quite vocal. At the first of these meetings, I remember one member leaving quite abruptly, as we moved from scriptural reflection to prayer, and later sending a note saying that Bible reading and prayer were meant for Sunday mornings and shouldn't delay our getting down to the "business of the meeting." A few others sent word one way or another that they were uncomfortable with such doings and wouldn't be back unless we abandoned what they believed was an undertaking suitable only for priests. Despite this resistance, born no doubt from fear of uncertainty and change, the congregation as a whole was rallied by growing expectations of greater vitality ahead. Whether this community was built out of prayerfulness, or gratitude and prayerfulness grew out of this sense of community, I do not know.

When I agreed to be senior warden, I also sensed that I was being called to lead the search process for a new rector. I shared this intuition with the vestry, and they agreed that I should become co-chair of the search committee, along with another parishioner whose family roots were well grounded in the parish. Our vision from the start was to have a search committee whose process could be a model for the church community we were hoping for: born of prayerfulness, guided by careful listening to our own hearts and to each other, and acting by consensus with mutual love and respect.

We were assisted in this by a very able consultant who was herself contemplatively grounded, with an advanced degree in pastoral psychology. Throughout the search process, she played a very important role of gently keeping our egos in check and reminding us to be open to the Spirit at all times, but especially when we gathered to reflect and discern as best we could what was called for next. She accomplished this remarkable feat by facilitating the formation of our own "rules" of conduct for the process and then holding us to them. Among these helpful rules were, No interruptions when someone else is speaking; take a moment to reflect before you speak; and anyone may call for a respite when the group seems at odds or confused. While these meeting rules can easily be justified in secular culture as promoting positive group dynamics, they resonate strongly with the guiding principles of group spiritual direction where the intent is to make space for listening and responding to the Spirit. Our consultant was also very helpful to me privately by assuming the functions of a spiritual director; she prayed with and for our committee and for my prayerfulness; she helped me relax into the process and let God guide; and she very adroitly assisted my own discernment of where my personal needs and ego were getting in the way. Our spiritual friendship has lasted to this day, and we try to meet over a meal quarterly to renew our ties and share our journeys.

The search committee of twelve was chosen by the vestry to represent broadly the congregation with representation from young and elderly, lifelong parishioners and relative newcomers, those with young children and those who were grandparents, liturgical conservatives and some who liked liturgical variety, and some who resisted change and some who fervently desired change in one direction or another. In short, every conceivable point of view was represented on the committee. The parish had been through almost eighteen months of a self-study process before the search committee was appointed. In that process, we learned that there was a growing sense of lay ownership of the mission of the parish and a lot more flexibility about what the future might bring than many had thought possible. In short, the congregation was hopeful but anxious about losing what we each valued most while we were struggling to find a vision for the future. This was also the starting point for the search committee. In beginning its work, the search committee agreed that we would hear from two or three members at each meeting about what each hoped for and feared most as an outcome of the search process. This sharing was scheduled immediately after the opening prayer and Bible study so that it could be offered and listened to in a prayerful manner. Some, for whom such sharing was unfamiliar, were uncomfortable and appeared to give perfunctory responses or ones that reflected their own agendas. After a few breakthroughs in which intimate disclosures were treated with respect and vulnerability was honored, a climate of mutual trust began to emerge and eventually enveloped everyone on the committee.

Becoming prayerful together in our undertaking did not come easily in this diverse group. Several members continued until the very end of our work to resist time spent in silence, spontaneous prayer of any type, and the language of discernment. They believed that God had given them good minds and considerable talents that should be applied forthwith to the selection process, with God's will defined as a majority vote. A larger group began with this assumption but was persuaded by our study and discussion of discernment and the formation of consensus that perhaps there were better ways for spiritual communities to reach a decision with which all could be comfortable. But a growing majority of the committee came to see our task as one of discernment on behalf of our broader community rather than an executive job search. And it was this sentiment that guided our process. How did this come about? In looking back, I would have to say it was the work of the Spirit. The seeds that the consultant and I had tried to plant were a quiet confidence in a Spirit-led process, the willingness to spend our precious time together in prayer and listening, and an unqualified commitment to each other as potential voices of God in the process.

So, were we successful in our undertaking a prayerful search process? More recently I've had the opportunity to witness an executive search undertaken by the Shalem Institute. This is an ecumenical Christian spiritual formation center that offers extension courses and programs grounded in contemplative thought and practices. Their search committee and board were of one mind and heart about the need for a Spirit-led process rooted in prayer and openness. While there must have been disagreements, trust and confidence and mutual respect from a shared vision of discernment abounded from the beginning and thus rendered superfluous much of the time my church search committee spent moving toward common ground and building our trust of each other and of God's guidance. We almost certainly never reached the solidarity of purpose and vision achieved by an organization like Shalem, but as we reached the hard decisions late in the process, God must have smiled on our faithfulness. Even now, some four years after we finished our work, an indelible bond forged from the grace of the prayerful road we trod, albeit imperfectly, is still palpable among those most committed to the process.

What, then, has been learned from these sometimes fumbling efforts to bring to the surface and nurture a spirit of prayerfulness in the life of a congregation in transition? In looking back now, it appears that I must have been a little crazy to embark on such a course with as little training and background as I had at the time. But my three years' experience in Shalem's group spiritual direction program had empowered my vision of how a spiritual community ought to function. There is little doubt the efforts might have fallen on barren ground were it not for the strong support of my retiring rector and of staunch church supporters of our transition efforts. Some of the latter were church friends of similar persuasion, and others were just following the lead in trust that God would take us in the right direction. I am grateful to both. And of course it has occurred to me that the Spirit may have had some role in emboldening our vision and plans.

A second learning from the experience is that the support of spiritual friends is essential for perseverance. In my situation, I was blessed with a nucleus of spiritual friends in the parish and a consultant-facilitator for the process who was well grounded in prayerfulness and discernment. Each played uniquely valuable roles in providing personal and group support during difficult times. My Shalem spiritual direction group supported me personally in prayer, which was enormously strengthening, and on some occasions added their prayers for difficult issues in the transition. At the time, I was reluctant to draw them into a process that I had not then discerned as a calling. Now I would be inclined to invoke their prayers more regularly.

Another lesson modeled in group spiritual direction and rediscovered here was that one can trust the group's process when it's infused with prayerfulness. When others sense or discern from their experience that the process is not being driven by private agendas and is inclusive, since no one has a monopoly on the Spirit, resistance fades into the background. For some, it will be willing acquiescence but without a full buy-in; in time, this can change to a warm embrace of the process and noticeable personal transformation. For others, the moment may not be ripe for such openness because of serious unresolved personal agendas or because of old wounds that haven't healed. A few will protest loudly as they respond to fears of change or loss of influence, but a prayerful group can usually discern these motives and either discount them or reach out to those so afflicted.

A final observation is that many people are receptive to, if not hungry for, a more overtly spiritual grounding for what they do in their parish churches. At least this was true in my small, traditional Episcopal church where little but our liturgy was held in common. A new language was required to speak to each other about encounters with the holy. In our case, the language was to change again with the advent of a new rector, but now the centrality of praying for each other and listening for God's call to us is on the table for all to see and embrace.

Just as it is possible for a single person to assemble and instruct small groups in the discipline of spiritual direction rooted in intercessory prayer, the attributes of prayerfulness and openness to God can be birthed in larger groups of bonded individuals. Attitudes and practices may change only in a small subset who understand and faithfully respond, but the fruits of the process can extend to the whole and beyond.

III.

====

Group Spiritual Direction with Clergy

In considering making group spiritual direction available for clergy, the question often arises, "Should we offer clergy-only groups or invite clergy to join mixed groups?" It's obvious that there are pros and cons to both possibilities. Some clergy come to group spiritual direction at Shalem because they prefer to be in heterogeneous groups. About half the clergy who come to our Spiritual Life of Spiritual Leaders Conference/Retreat, when given the option of being in an all-clergy group or a mixed group, choose a mixed group. They say, among other things, that it's too easy to slide into "shop talk" when they are with only clergy. At the same time, there are clergy who say that they prefer to be in an all-clergy group because they feel they can trust the feedback from the other group members more if they have been in similar situations. They also say it would be hard to bring some of their issues to a mixed group for fear of shocking some people in the group.

The two essays that follow this are about doing group spiritual direction with clergy-only groups. I will offer a few generic observations on this and some things I have learned from my own experience that seemed to work with clergy-only groups. Again I remind you that your own prayerful discernment is needed before you make a decision about what you will do. As a facilitator, no matter what your decision is, you will need to be sure that participants want to share the intent of group spiritual direction and are willing and able to honor the process. Once having agreed to facilitate a group, you will need to relinquish all your presuppositions and management skills so that you can be freely available to God for what might be called for moment by moment.

Spiritual direction at its best is about being in touch with and noticing God in all of life. Eventually, most of one's life comes into the conversation of spiritual direction. In clergy-only groups it is easy to focus primarily on one's "professional role" to the exclusion of one's own prayer, family life, friends, or whatever else might be part of one's life. When that happens, a question such as, "What happens when you pray about this?" might invite people to talk about their prayer. A question like, "How does what you are describing fit with how God seems to be present for you in other parts of your life?" may remind the person that God is not confined to one's "professional" role; it may also encourage people to talk about other parts of their lives in the group.

Groups in which people talk mostly about their "professional roles" often move from the intent of group spiritual direction into more general discussion of common issues and sharing of solutions. In particular, people in clergy-only groups often seem to find it easier to revert to their helping modes than to be a prayerful presence for one another, listening in silence for the leading of the Spirit. Here, the facilitator might invite the group into silence for a few minutes, then ask those who first raised the issues if they have any sense of what God might be wanting to say to them through all the words they are hearing. In any type of group, it can be helpful for the facilitator to begin sessions by reminding people of why they are together and inviting them to notice when they seem to be getting off track.

It could be difficult for clergy to be vulnerable with one another, to share their doubts and fears and those parts of their lives, including (maybe especially) their prayer, where they feel they are being less than "successful." This may be especially true when clergy are in the same denomination and may be in competition with each other for promotions. It also can be true when clergy who see each other frequently in other settings or work together are in the same group. Sometimes mixing clergy from different denominations or at least from different geographical areas may eliminate this occupational hazard. It also may be appropriate to ask participants if there is anyone they know applying to be in a group with whom they would rather not be. Groups where facilitators can share vulnerably with the group, especially in the initial get-acquainted, faith-sharing time and the process time at the end of each session, usually move into an open, trusting space more quickly.

The same thing that has been said of clergy groups for spiritual direction might also be said of other professional groupings, and perhaps even of staffs that want to be together in group spiritual direction. As in spiritual direction in general or group spiritual direction particularly, the bottom-line considerations must center on the freedom to be oneself in the group, that is, to be able to say what is given in prayer to say and to trust God's Spirit at work in the process. What matters, then, is not whether we offer heterogeneous or homogeneous groups, but rather, which will better serve the intent of those coming to group spiritual direction. And, equally as important, "How is God inviting me, as a facilitator, to participate in the ministry of group spiritual direction?"

Rose Mary Dougherty

Learning with a Clergy Group

Don Kelley

The spiritual direction group I facilitate includes five pastors from the same denomination, and we've met monthly since early 1998. What am I learning from this experience—my first as a facilitator for group direction—and what are my unanswered questions?

My responses to these two questions are the central messages of this essay, supplemented with a profile of our group, sources of support for me in the facilitating role, and other details to give a clear picture of the experience.

To protect the privacy of group members, I have omitted identifying details such as their denomination and place names. Members' names are fictitious, of course, and I have made other alterations in the interest of keeping the members anonymous. I add my deep gratitude for their presence in the group, their willing participation, and their consistent praying, during and between group meetings.

My becoming the facilitator of the clergy group started with these events:

- Taking a six-month sabbatical in 1986 with my wife for rest and openness to grace. As human service professionals, we were depleted from too much availability to others and not enough availability to ourselves and to God.

- Choosing a Catholic priest as my spiritual director. This helped me discern a call to be a spiritual director.

- Completing the Shalem Institute's Spiritual Guidance Program and experiencing, so far, more than 100 group spiritual direction sessions with members of my local spiritual directors peer group. In this group, one or two members at monthly meetings describe awarenesses, concerns, and questions about their own relationship with God from being the spiritual director for a particular (and anonymous) person. The group member presenting asks the others to join in discerning the presence and guidance of the Spirit in the sharing. Our peer group becomes a community for discernment during these monthly meetings and is a specialized version of general group spiritual direction, as described in this essay.

- Formally offering individual spiritual direction for clergy and lay persons.

In addition, group psychotherapy and a twelve-step program helped me become freer psychologically and spiritually, more available to God, myself, and others. Retreats also helped prepare me to facilitate spiritual direction groups. I take retreats for rest and spiritual renewal and co-lead contemplative retreats and quiet days for clergy. I also train clergy and lay leaders in designing and leading retreats through Stillpoint Ministries, an ecumenical spiritual formation ministry.

On the way to facilitating group spiritual direction, I began to notice two emerging attractions. First, I marveled at the varied and powerful ways that the Holy Spirit worked in and among the members of my spiritual directors peer group when we gathered as a community for discernment each month. I wanted more of this graced group experience. And, second, I felt attracted to work with clergy. I tried to understand this attraction — was it the influence of my brother's years as a Catholic priest, my service with pastors of many denominations on the Christian Council of Metropolitan Atlanta, or the more recent spiritual friendships with clergy directees in individual direction? I've stopped trying to understand; I accept the attraction now as Spirit guided.

Notices from Shalem about groups for spiritual direction and of the publication of Rose Mary Dougherty's book on group direction also influenced me. Being invited to serve on a Quaker Clearness Committee boosted my attraction to groups for discernment. The prayerful silence, attention to the theme (vocational, in this case) presented by the focus person, and the unrushed questioning for clearness of this group model, though not overtly spiritual direction, was profoundly spiritual for me.

I began to talk with peers about group direction and imagined myself as a facilitator. I brought these awarenesses and attractions to prayer, asking to know what to say or do. An answer came through a clergy peer, a former directee. This friend linked me with a senior pastor interested in spiritual direction, who agreed to gather a group of clergy associates for an exploration with me of group direction.

The senior pastor and I planned the meeting; six clergy attended, told of their interests in continuing spiritual formation, and asked questions about individual and group direction. My follow-up letter to the senior pastor presented four options based on what I heard at the meeting: individual direction only; individual direction for some and group for others; group direction only; and quiet days or guided reading and discussion. From their questions and comments in the meeting, I sensed low readiness of the pastors for group direction. Was it *my* lack of readiness I was sensing—my unreadiness to step out in my first facilitating role? The Holy Spirit had a clear direction for us. To my surprise, the pastors chose the option of group direction only, and five of the six pastors joined the group with an agreement to try it for four months. In February 1998, we had our first group meeting, with an introduction to the desired prayerfulness process and rhythm of our times together. I shared a draft of proposed group guidelines and asked for additions or other changes to be discussed at our next group meeting. Members had no proposed changes, so we adopted the guidelines with the understanding that changes could be proposed whenever one of us sensed the need. Our group was forming!

Learning with a Clergy Group

A small church with almost no activity during the week became the setting for our monthly morning sessions. The location was quiet and convenient for all but me; I had a sixty-mile drive to reach the church. The drive became another gift; the hour going to the group gave me extra time for opening to the Holy Spirit as primary director and for praying for each group member, including myself. The trip home usually included reflection on the group experience, gratitude, and more intercessory prayer.

After losing access to the small church, we tested meeting in a large, busy church. The noise of people talking outside our meeting room distracted us. Easy access of church staff and members to their pastor, a group member, disrupted the prayerful flow of our group time. We are meeting again in the original small, quiet church, having learned how essential quiet and freedom from interruptions are for group direction.

Only two of the original five group members continue with the group, which again has five members—one a female pastor. We have had nine different members in our three years of meeting: one member retired and three moved to churches in distant locations.

The group is homogeneous in its shared denominational affiliation and tradition, and diverse in spiritual practices, discernment themes, age (from thirty to sixty), and pastoral responsibilities (from serving two small rural churches with no paid staff to being senior pastors of larger, well-staffed churches).

Some of the group members use journaling, one developed and follows a spiritual rule of life, another takes quiet days alone

135

and with other clergy, and some see their sermon preparation as a primary spiritual practice.

Discernment themes include vocational change questions (one member felt called to missionary work); spiritual restlessness and an awareness of not enough availability to self and God; conflicts in parish relationships; personal and family health concerns with implications for their ministry; and themes of deep gratitude and consolation.

We are not the same group all the time—members move, usually in the summer months—so we are evolving ways to add a member when one leaves. We ask about the right timing for an addition, and we pray for guidance, staying open to the surprises of the Holy Spirit. We name potential new group members. I talk to those we sense are ready for group direction—describing our process, listening to what they long for in personal spiritual deepening, reviewing the guidelines, and inviting them to visit a group session. Our prayer frames the discernment and guides our actions. So far, this approach is working for us. However, since most changes are in the summer, we might meet only between October and June to get more group continuity.

Previous group spiritual direction experience did not prevent my surprise and frustration over some of the challenges and my slowness in finding workable responses and clear lessons. These initial six challenges and associated lessons have been a mixed blessing, combining uncertainty and occasional anguish with welcome clarity and even consolation. Often fear and worry were my first responses to the challenges; not much early praying or other calls for help, I'm sad to say.

Opening to the Sources of Trust

Here is an example: Paul arrived for our group session full of anger and tension over conflict in his congregation. He wanted our group response to a letter he planned to give his congregation. Members asked how the conflict started and suggested solutions. I sensed the request as a distraction, not the "stuff" of spiritual direction. I called a pause for guidance. From the silence, I became aware of my fear that problem solving, a frequent challenge in our group, would dominate our discerning. I was not trusting the Holy Spirit, our group members, or myself to find God in the letter, in our friend's anger and tension. I shared my awarenesses, and we chose to hear Paul's letter. We heard the compassion and anger in the letter and joined as co-discerners with Paul to find God in the parish conflict and in Paul's longing to express his truth to the congregation in love. Some members offered to comment on the politics of the situation and counsel Paul after our group meeting. The grace of it all was truly amazing.

Lesson: Trust the Holy Spirit, myself, the members, the learning going on in the group, and the essential wisdom of the group. Group spiritual direction is not meant to be rigid, closed to the Spirit, or to the good judgment of facilitators and group members.

Slowness in Telling or Asking About Praying

Members do not often tell how they are praying in or about an experience they present, and few questions about praying are asked of presenters. Prayer experience is considered very personal, and members resist a question such as, "What happens in your prayer about that?" The more emotional the sharing, the less likely praying and prayer are included. Why is this? Do the presenter and listening members get so caught up in the feelings associated with the shared event that they lose the focus on relationship with God and on prayer? That may have happened when Mary (with obvious disturbance and tears) told of a male lay leader stomping out of church just as she started her sermon. The man later said he had never had a woman preacher and would not accept one now. How do we get more attention to prayer, especially in emotionally charged experiences?

Lesson: Talking in the group about resistance to prayer questions and the appropriateness of them in noticing movements of the Spirit seems to lessen the resistance. I model asking about prayer experiences, hoping members will do the same, but the change is very slow. Initially I did not call for silence and invite all of us to open in prayer for more attention to prayer and more willingness to trust one another with disclosure and questions about prayer. I'm more likely to take that facilitating action now. Also, I did not show the group direction video with the clergy group. Doing so is very likely to prompt more attention to prayer.

There is a larger awareness here, a most important one: We can always be open to a presenter's sharing—indeed our entire time together—as prayer. Surely Mary's tearful lament about the hurtful challenge to her presence in the pulpit—to her identity—was prayer, though the words *praying* and *prayer* were not used.

To deepen our prayerfulness, I sometimes choose scripture passages and short meditations as an invitation to open to God's longing for us and our longing for God. With these, we experience a growing safety of our group as a place to share spiritual consolations and desolations, joys and sorrows—what really matters most in relation to God. Another time, when a boost seemed necessary to welcome more direct sharing about relationships with God, I asked the members, "What is your spiritual growing edge?" This short question facilitated direct sharing that enriched the group session. I caution the reader and myself here; too much of this prompting by the group facilitator can interfere with the movement of the Spirit in the slow search by members for words to express their longing or their joy in relation to God.

Embracing Different Prayer Practices

I was unprepared for the preference of the pastors to say prayers aloud for one another, and I interpreted it as a distraction rather than a difference in our traditions. I preferred silent to spoken prayer and was troubled until I asked in prayer for guidance, which freed me to be more open to their spontaneous and love-filled spoken prayer.

Lesson: The Spirit moves as the Spirit chooses, not as I choose. I began to be open to the graced moments in the pastors' spoken prayer and now join in as I feel prompted. Spoken prayer boosts the general prayerfulness of our sessions and affirms a traditional prayer form of group members. The challenge became a blessing.

139

Waiting Through Discomfort with Silence

At a recent group meeting, the silence between presentations seemed full of tension. I sensed that one or both of the members who had not presented were wrestling over what to present and even whether to present. Finally, one member began to share, and the tension released. After ending our session, the presenter said, "Don, I was hoping you would save me by breaking that long silence; now I'm glad you waited." My waiting in the silence and tension helped members embrace the silence.

Lesson: Wait, then wait some more before trying to "improve upon the silence."

Sharing When Group Members
Have Similar Roles and Experiences

Each member of our clergy group experiences conflict between pastoral availability to others and finding time for self and God. One member expressed a shared lament about not taking enough time for rest and renewal, saying:

> When I was in staff ministries, I took retreats and what I called mental health days. In the past twenty years as a pastor, I've rarely done that. I get four weeks of vacation and have never taken more than two. I get a day off a week, but I typically spend it working in my office at home or still running to the hospital or such.

Another member told of having his family vacations frequently interrupted by calls to return for a funeral or other critical events among parishioners. Problem solving in our group is more likely when members share these kinds of experiences, since the others in the group have similar responsibilities and experiences.

Lesson: Disclosures by clergy of pastoral demands and difficulties can draw the group into sharing experiences and searching for solutions, into a group for mutual support rather than a community for discernment. We talk in the group of this potential distraction from our prayerfulness and our being spiritual directors for one another. I use articles, book recommendations, and memos to the members to respond to topics from the group experience best handled outside the group, but I choose to trust our "community for discernment" much more than these.

Asking Facilitators To Do More Than Facilitate Group Direction

Being asked for articles and books on Christian spirituality is one of many requests that may go beyond facilitation. The drivenness, the emphasis by pastors on availability to others, prompts more than one of our group members to ask for current reading on Christian spirituality that may speak to their need. How to respond and stay in the facilitator role?

Lesson: Usually I respond to individual needs, avoid a dependence on written material, ask the members for their own preferred sources, and encourage all of us to keep bringing these requests to prayer—especially me, the former teacher, vulnerable to choosing multiple roles and thereby confusing group members. I do have a few favorites that I offer from time to time. *Soul Feast: An Invitation to the Christian Spiritual Life* by Marjorie Thompson is an introductory book I like. The book has chapters on spiritual yearning, prayer, spiritual direction, and on hospitality and developing a rule of life, but I hesitate telling about this book, about doing this "resourcing." I urge those asking for book titles to begin their own book, a journal with their questions, concerns, happiness, and fears, and their reflections on scripture and poems and other inspiring messages. I continue looking for resources that respond to the members' requests, wondering whether or not to share what I find. Two articles that met recent requests are Gerald May's "Contemplative Spiritual Formation: An Introduction" in the *Shalem News* of December 1994 and Janet Ruffing's "Resisting the Demon of Busyness" in the Summer 1995 issue of *Spiritual Life*.

I feel fortunate and grateful to be supported as a facilitator by a peer in this ministry who facilitates two clergy groups. She also has facilitated parish spiritual direction groups for two years of monthly group meetings. We share our challenges and lessons and pray for one another.

Monthly participation in group direction with my spiritual director colleagues is another steady support for me. Here I experience again and again being a member in group direction. Our group is truly a community for discernment.

These questions come out of this first group facilitating experience:

- Should individual spiritual direction be a prerequisite for joining a spiritual direction group? My current answer is *No*, from the experience with this clergy group where no one has individual spiritual direction experience. I prefer to offer more help in calling attention to discussion and problem solving, in the need for silence, and in careful waiting for signs of readiness by the presenter for another comment or question that comes with experience in spiritual direction.

- When to begin a discussion of my leaving the group and for the members to continue by sharing the facilitating role? I'm not ready to leave. Am I too attached to this amazing, committed, and loving group of pastors and the many consolations flowing from the Spirit's actions among us? Appropriate attachment seems essential in the start-up of a group, but when does the attachment inhibit the maturing of the group and the facilitator's personal spiritual deepening?

- What is the meaning of my occasional memos to the group members (about fifteen in three years)? Is it a control mechanism for me—a fear that without it the group will die (and I will have failed)? I question this practice now and wonder if there is ever a place for written messages to group members about anything other than group guidelines and schedules.

Don Kelley

A *continuing grace* from the clergy group experience is my enthusiasm for being with the members, the frequent flow of prayers for them, and the steady prompting of my own spiritual deepening from their disclosures and discernments. When members report increases in spiritual freedom for opening to the Spirit's movement in their pastoral ministry, I rejoice. What great gifts of discerning and learning each of us is being given!

Group Spiritual Direction with Clergy

Lois Lindbloom

Introduction

For the past two years, I have facilitated group spiritual direction with groups of clergy in my community, Northfield, Minnesota. In the first year, two groups of four members each met monthly for two and one-half hours from September through May. In the second year, three groups, two with four participants and one with three, met for the same length of time. These twelve ministers made up about one-third of the members of the local ministerial association, a group that meets monthly and whose members cooperate with one another regarding various community concerns. Several denominations were represented, all Christian.

Facilitating the groups has given me great satisfaction. It has been an example of true vocation as described by Frederich

Buechner: "The place God calls you to is the place where your deep gladness and the world's deep hunger meet."[1]

I was introduced to group spiritual direction at a Shalem workshop. I had recently completed Shalem's two-year program in spiritual guidance, was active as a spiritual director for individuals, and met monthly in a peer supervision group for spiritual directors. The brochure offering the opportunity to learn more about spiritual direction in a group setting was inviting to me.

In retrospect, my decision to offer spiritual direction groups for clergy does not seem surprising. In the local church and in the larger Baptist denomination of which I am a part, I have worked with clergy in many settings over the years. Professionally, as a psychologist, I have facilitated groups of various kinds, and I appreciate the contributions that individuals give and receive in groups. My own spiritual journey has often been nurtured in small group settings. A few years before attending the Shalem group spiritual direction workshop, I had written an academic paper on group mysticism as found in the Quaker tradition. All of these experiences converged for me in the Shalem group spiritual direction workshop.

One of the questions discussed among the workshop participants was, "How might we bring this information and experience to our home settings?" I heard, especially from clergy, "I wish there were a group like this in which I could participate." I returned to my home to pray about and discern whether I might bring group spiritual direction to clergy in my community.

Eugene H. Peterson, a pastor, teacher, and writer, helped confirm for me the value of spiritual direction for pastors:

What are the actual means by which I carry out this pastoral vocation, this ordained ministry, this professional commitment to God's word and God's grace in my life and in the lives of the people to whom I preach and give the sacraments, among whom I command a life for others in the name of Jesus Christ? What connects these great realities of God and the great realities of salvation to the geography of this parish and to the chronology of this week? The answer among the masters whom I consult doesn't change: a trained attentiveness to God in prayer, in Scripture reading, in spiritual direction. This has not been tried and discarded because it didn't work, but tried and found difficult (and more than a bit tedious) and so shelved in favor of something or other that could be fit into a busy pastor's schedule.[2]

My next step was to talk with my own pastor, who is active in the ministerial association. He told me that at the association's recent retreat the guest speaker was a spiritual director who introduced them to this practice, and he encouraged me to extend an invitation to the group.

My pastor's support for this venture remained strong at each step of the way. I am certain his endorsement of the idea among his colleagues encouraged them to participate. At the introductory meeting, he brought our attention to Luke 5:1–7 and suggested that this was an opportunity to go deeper in our walk with God: "Put out into the deep water…" (Luke 5:4).

Lois Lindbloom

Invitation

A copy of the invitation sent to association members can be found in Appendix A. Receiving the invitation in the spring allowed participants the summer to consider the offer and to have sufficient information for making a commitment for the fall. The descriptions were meant to give enough details to make the choice clear to the reader. Some conclusions regarding size of the groups and general parameters of meeting times were stated in this initial communication to eliminate awkward situations later—for instance, if two people came, would the group still be offered? Or, if someone wanted to be a part of the group but was only available in the evenings, could he or she be a part of the group? Finding common times for a group to meet was one of the challenges of this process. Narrowing the variables from the beginning helped make it a bit easier.

Introductory Meeting

Group spiritual direction as developed at the Shalem Institute builds on three foundational principles:

1. *Spiritual Direction.* Spiritual direction is an ongoing conversation between a participant and a spiritual director in which they watch and listen together for the direction of the Spirit in the participant's life. It is a spiritual discipline or practice. It is something one does to turn to God, to deliberately pay attention to one's walk with God. The goal is to become more aware of and

responsive to the presence of God in one's life. Key questions in spiritual direction are these: "Where is God in this part of your life? What happens when you pray about this part of your life?"

2. *Spiritual Community.* Jesus said that when two or three gather together in Christ's name, God is present (Matt 18:20). The Christian understanding of spiritual community is further inspired by the Apostle Paul's metaphor of the church as the body of Christ (1 Cor 12:12–27). Each member of the body is unique and important, and all members are interdependent. Group spiritual direction recognizes the need of each member for the others and the unique presence of God in purposefully meeting together.

The purpose of being together is prayer. Group spiritual direction is not a therapy group, an advice-giving group, or a support group for people who have a common concern. It is a community of people meeting to watch and listen for the Spirit of God present in each person. Each is present with the others, supporting that part of life where each is alone with God. The goal is to be more aware of and responsive to God in one's life.

3. *Intercessory Prayer.* Intercessory prayer is a willingness to stay in the presence of God on behalf of another. Unlike petitions that begin with stating what the pray-er wants from God, this prayer begins by listening for what God's desire may be. It is grounded in Jesus' prayer, "Thy will be done." Four questions help the pray-ers set aside their own desires and listen for God's will:

- God, what is your deepest desire for this person?

- God, what do you want my prayer to be?

149

- God, is there anything in me that is getting in the way of my joining your prayer for this person?

- God, is there anything you want me to say or do on your behalf for this person?

(Questions are taken from Rose Mary Dougherty's book, *Group Spiritual Direction: Community for Discernment*.)

The Shalem model of group spiritual direction reflects the contemplative tradition of Christian spirituality, including times of silence. Silence allows the participants to pay attention to the Spirit of God without interruption. Silence allows each participant to move beyond immediate, usual ways of responding and consider what may be shared with the group from the moments of silent prayer.

In our introductory meeting, these three principles were presented and portions of Shalem's video on group spiritual direction were reviewed. The group also participated in a time of silent prayer using the four intercessory prayer questions mentioned.

What were the thoughts and desires of the clergy who came to hear more about group spiritual direction? A few had been in spiritual direction in the past and were looking for a renewal of that spiritual practice. Some said ministry was going well but was taking its toll on the minister: continual service for others without sustained spiritual nourishment for oneself looked like a pathway to burnout. A few said they had no one with whom they regularly talked about their own walk with God. Another said this invitation seemed to be an answer to prayer in the middle of a difficult

situation. Some said it was hard to pray alone and they were looking for support for prayer. In one minister's denomination, group
spiritual direction had been recommended for all clergy. Another
reported that, when he came to this community, he had determined to seek out some sort of group in which he could be honest about his own spiritual life.[3] Most were unfamiliar with group
spiritual direction and were curious.

In this first introductory meeting, participants were given a
form on which to respond if they wished to be in a group. They also
wrote their preferences for three possible meeting times and noted
anyone in the room with whom they preferred not to be in a group.
All seven who came signed up for a group. One other minister
expressed an interest but was unavailable for the meeting; that person signed up a few days later. In the second year, a letter of invitation was sent to all association members again. No introductory
meeting was held. Instead, the orientation to group spiritual direction occurred in the first meeting of groups in which new members
were present. One group kept the same membership both years.

Besides finding a common meeting time that works, the
other challenge in setting up a group is the group composition.
Participants need to be in a group where they have freedom to
speak about their own lives and to be open to God on behalf of
others. For this reason, members of the same staff requested not
to be in a group together, and in all groups this pattern has been
maintained.

Confidentiality was emphasized from the beginning. We
would not share information from within the group with anyone
outside the group. In the first meeting of each group, we

expanded the meaning of confidentiality. We agreed that the time set aside for the group was a prayerful place where participants gave each other permission to participate in one another's life stories in a unique way. However, that did not give permission to resume the conversation in other places such as the grocery store or on the phone. We would not talk about the content of the group elsewhere unless specifically invited to do so by the person whose story it was. Finally, I asked if the participants were comfortable telling people outside the group who was in the group. On this question, one group concluded they would be comfortable having that information shared; the other groups chose to keep the group roster confidential.

Group Meetings

> Hospitality wants to offer friendship without binding
> the guest and freedom without leaving him alone.
> Hospitality is not to change people, but to offer them
> space where change can take place.[4]

All group meetings were in my home, which is in a quiet, rural setting, a ten-minute drive from Northfield. The two and one-half hour meetings began with a social time in the kitchen, chatting with one another over coffee, tea, and quick bread. And laughing! In most gatherings, there was humor and laughter. After about fifteen minutes, we moved to the meeting room where I read a brief selection, often a few verses of scripture. Then we observed fifteen minutes of silence.

A few months into the group, one of the participants said, "I need all of the steps in order to arrive at this place of prayer-fulness. I need the drive out here, leaving behind the church and my work. I need the gathering in the kitchen to reconnect with the other people in the group. I need to hear the reading to focus my attention. And, I need the fifteen minutes of silence to settle into quiet, to a place of listening, to being here."

The late Douglas Steere wrote a similar account of prayer. This quotation is one of the readings I used in the groups as a focus before the time of silence:

> The first of these rules (of prayer) is that in order to pray, you have to stop being "too elsewhere" and to *be there*.…You have to care enough about this placing of yourself in an act of absolute receptivity to the Divine, that what is at the heart of things may take possession of you, mind, heart, and will. You have to care enough so that you will collect yourself, move back into your own soul from the distant suburbs where much of life tends to be spent, and honestly be there.[5]

I have learned that the reading must be short. Members of one group still tease me about the reading I once offered that left them confused and less focused than they had been before the reading. It was too long (about two paragraphs), unfamiliar, and too complicated. (I suggested that this might be instructive to them about what it is like to listen to a long sermon.) I always read the selection two or three times. The reading often came from my own time of meditation with scripture in the previous month. Some examples:

> He gives power to the faint,
>> and strengthens the powerless.
> Even youths will faint and be weary,
>> and the young will fall exhausted;
> but those who wait for the LORD shall renew their
>>> strength,
>> they shall mount up with wings like eagles,
> they shall run and not be weary,
>> they shall walk and not faint. (Isa 40:29–31)

> Do not be like a horse or a mule, without under-
>>> standing,
>> whose temper must be curbed with bit and bridle,
>> else it will not stay near you.
> I will instruct you and teach you the way you
>>> should go;
> I will counsel you with my eye upon you.
>> (Ps 32:9, 8)

Be still, and know that I am God! (Ps 46:10)

The grip of the usual is what must be broken.... Solitude and silence are sure to do it.[6]

The function of prayer is to change my own mind, to put on the mind of Christ, to enable grace to break into me.[7]

The readings were always followed by about fifteen minutes of silence. Some participants said that in the first meetings this time seemed long, but that later, the bell ending the silence rang too soon. Sometimes people reported being restless during the silence; sometimes they commented on the rich gift of that quiet time.

After the time of silence, following the Shalem model, each person was given about ten minutes in turn to talk about her or his own life and walk with God in the past month. As facilitator, my role was to keep the structure of the process in place so the participants could listen prayerfully to one another without undue concern about the time and the process. After each ten-minute turn, we spent two or three minutes in silence, considering the intercessory prayer questions on behalf of the one who just spoke: God, what is your deepest desire for this person? God, what do you want my prayer for him or her to be? God, is there something in me that I need to surrender, to let go, because it is interfering with my joining your prayer for this person? God, is there anything you want me to say on your behalf to him or her?

Then, out of that prayer, group members spoke what came to them. Many times I also offered something. After ten minutes of response time, we spent about two minutes praying silently for the person and allowing her or him time to consider what had been offered from the group. In this way, we listened to two people, then took a brief break, followed by two more people. If someone was absent, we prayed for that person, also.

After listening to a presentation, I sometimes felt the need to remind all of us of the intercessory prayer questions. I came to realize that even though those questions had been a focus since the beginning and participants often spoke about how valuable they were, they were not an automatic way of responding for any of us. One group member said, "I feel like I'm still way back there on the learning curve." So, I reminded us of the questions periodically. On other occasions, I felt such a strong urge myself to give advice or to reassure someone or to tell my own story as a guide to someone else, that I repeated the questions in part to bring myself back to that place of intercessory prayer.

On one occasion a group member spoke about one of the current, big, controversial topics of church and theology. It was hard for all of us not to get caught up in the issue and to lose sight of staying in the presence of God on behalf of that individual. By being reminded of the intercessory prayer questions, and by taking time in silence to listen for the Spirit's presence, the group stayed "on track" as a spiritual director. In the reflection time at the end of the group meeting, that person said she had not wanted the group to get into the issue itself; she had wanted a place to discern God's specific desire for her. If they had not been called back to the questions, I suspect the group might have interfered with her discernment rather than encouraging it.

At the end of each group session, we spent about five minutes reflecting on our time together. Primarily we asked, How were we with one another today? Was there anything that seemed to get in the way of our prayerfulness with one another? Was there anything that seemed to be particularly supportive of our prayerfulness? This time also gave participants an opportunity to comment briefly on the meeting, for example, "I'm glad we were all present today," or "This was like an oasis in my week."

The suggested contributions were placed in a basket near the entrance of the meeting room. After the first meeting or two, some of the ministers brought a check from their church. My understanding of this is that they thought the group experience contributed to the ministry of their church and was worthy of the church's support.

When each group finished the nine-month series of gatherings, I wrote a few notes, especially regarding my role as facilitator, the group process, and specific prayer concerns for the participants. In those moments, I often became aware of how their lives and participation related in some way to my own walk with God.

Mentoring

Since the beginning of the groups, I have had a Shalem mentor with whom I have talked on the phone once every month or two about the groups. Three significant benefits came to me through having a mentor. First, I knew my mentor was praying for me, that I was supported through intercessory prayer while I sat with others who were praying for one another. Second, I knew I could talk with someone who had more experience in this process than I. Just knowing there was someone available with the wisdom of experience was reassuring to me. Third, our conversations and my own preparation for them often brought clarity and/or new ways of thinking about some issue.

Three specific examples stand out for me. In my first conversations with my mentor, he reminded me that my role was to be prayerful and to help the group honor the process. That was his response to my long, detailed, enthusiastic description about setting up the groups and the first meetings! As time went on, I often returned to that simple touchstone, recalling the importance of remaining faithful in those two things—prayer and honoring the process.

Another time I told my second mentor that I was concerned about whether I talked too much in the response time of the groups. After listening a while, she wondered what I did with my concern. I told her more about my thoughts. Back and forth we went. Finally, in her clearest question yet, she asked how I had prayed about my concern. I was quiet. Then I laughed at my own "blind spot." I had not prayed about my concern. Instead I had been trying to figure it out, fussing about it. I needed another person in my life to help me pay attention to what God's desire might be, just as members of the group helped one another listen for God's presence in their lives.

In another discussion with my mentor, she raised a question that I carried with me as I met with the groups in the next month. In the meetings it became clearer that I disagreed with her suggestion and was amused as I realized, "Even she may not be able to bridge this process to this place and these people the way I can."

Reflections

At the end of the next to the last meeting of the year, a handout (Appendix B) was given to members of the group. In the last meeting, participants verbally responded to the questions, either in their regular ten minutes of time or during slightly longer than usual reflections at the end. The handout was meant to invite responses that pertain to the purposes of group spiritual direction. For that reason, I reminded them of the foundations of group spiritual direction at the top of the handout. Also, while I wanted them to reflect on the year for their own sake and to share with the group, I did not want them to move into a critical, evaluative stance. Thus, the questions invited reflective responses.

I also have used this handout to introduce people to group spiritual direction. It seems to help people see the foundations quickly and clearly and invites consideration of whether this is an appropriate spiritual practice for them.

Several participants responded that the group helped their awareness of God's presence in their lives before, during, and after the meetings. As the scheduled day approached, some said they looked back over the month to reflect on the themes of their lives. Others waited to pay attention to what came forth in the meeting time. One participant said, "The group is a regular interval for 'breaching' into consciousness and speech whatever God has been doing in the depths, like a whale breaking the surface." Other comments about the group included the new and powerful experience of being prayed for by others; the feeling of acceptance and having something to contribute to others; the gift of spiritual community; and the preciousness of quiet time.

"I share a lament," one participant said. "You reflect. I don't get advice or have to fear that someone will feel the need to solve what I share. You listen for the voice of God. As the receiver of that prayer, I feel increasing freedom." Another person was on the track to burnout before the group, while yet another talked about the gift of sharing. "In my ministry I usually ask, 'What shall I say?' It was a wonderful relief that the question was, 'Is there anything you want me to say?' There is freedom not to have to say anything."

A next step for these groups would be for them to meet without an outside facilitator. One group considered that possibility for next year and decided to continue meeting without a facilitator for now. I am confident that they know the process well and will do fine. However, I have observed from the beginning that these are people whose job it is to be "in charge" in so many settings. They have commented on how good it is not to have to attend to the chairs, lights, and other logistics. Even the prayer questions give permission to not say anything. Having an outside facilitator who helps maintain the process does seem to enhance the freedom of participants to give and receive spiritual direction.

As I drive by the churches in my community, I pray for the pastors and their congregations. I do not recall doing that before these groups began. It is almost time to send out another invitation to the ministers. Many of the participants from last year have already said Yes to continuing. I am looking forward to another year of watching and listening together for the presence of God in our lives.

The author thanks the group participants for giving permission to use all direct and indirect quotations included in this chapter.

Notes

1. Frederich Buechner, *Wishful Thinking: A Theological ABC* (New York: Harper & Row, 1973), 95.

2. Eugene H. Peterson, *Working the Angles: The Shape of Pastoral Integrity* (Grand Rapids: Eerdmans, 1987), 16–17.
3. The groups included men and women. As I cite individual statements and reactions, I alternate between the masculine and feminine pronouns to preserve confidentiality.
4. Henri J. Nouwen, *Reaching Out: The Three Movements of the Spiritual Life* (New York: Doubleday, 1975), 51.
5. Douglas V. Steere, *Dimensions of Prayer* (New York: Harper & Row, 1962), 23.
6. Dallas Willard, *The Divine Conspiracy: Rediscovering Our Hidden Life in God* (San Francisco: Harper, 1998), 360.
7. Joan Chittister, O.S.B., *WomanStrength* (Kansas City: Sheed & Ward, 1990), 156.

Appendix A:
Group Spiritual Direction Opportunity for Northfield Clergy

Lois Lindbloom, spiritual director in Northfield, recently participated in a workshop on group spiritual direction through the Shalem Institute for Spiritual Formation in Bethesda, Maryland, and will be offering groups for clergy in the fall of 1998. Please consider joining and supporting other ministers in this spiritual discipline designed to encourage a deeper walk with God.

Spiritual Direction is an ongoing conversation between a participant and a spiritual director in which they watch and listen together for the direction of the Spirit in the participant's life. In *Group Spiritual Direction*, each individual experiences spiritual direction in the context of the group; the group becomes the spiritual director for one another. A facilitator provides structure to the group process. The goal is to become more aware of and responsive to the presence of God in one's life.

Expectation of Group Members:

1. Be available and committed to attend the meetings.
2. Pray for one another.
3. Be prayerfully present in the group, willing to be open to God on the behalf of another.
4. Be willing to share from your own story with others.
5. Hold all group information in confidence.

If This Invitation Interests You:

1. Please continue to pray about your decision to participate.
2. Watch for details about an introductory meeting in the fall.
3. You may contact Lois Lindbloom or Will Healy with your questions and/or reactions.
4. You may read a book and/or view a video on group spiritual direction, both produced by Shalem.

Details:

Following a two- to three-hour introductory meeting in the fall, if four or more wish to participate, a group or groups will be formed to meet monthly, 8–10 times, two and one-half hours each, on a weekday morning or afternoon, with Lois as facilitator, beginning in October. Suggested contribution for each meeting is $20; no one will be excluded for inability to contribute financially.

The primary role of a spiritual director is to pray, and this invitation comes as a result of my own prayer. Now that it is in writing and in your hands, I will continue to pray and trust that the Spirit of God will clearly nudge each of us to the right path for the fall.

Appendix B:
Reflections on
Group Spiritual Direction

As you prayerfully reflect on your experience of group spiritual direction, please do so with these foundations of group spiritual direction in mind:

Spiritual Direction. Spiritual direction is a spiritual discipline, an intentional action on my part to turn to God. Someone else joins me and helps me listen and watch for God's presence and direction in the story of my life.

Spiritual Community. Others in the body of Christ help me pay attention to my walk with God; in community my desire for God is expressed and heard; my response to God is nurtured and supported. Members of the group are present with one another, supporting that place where each is alone with God.

Intercessory Prayer. Prayer is rooted in listening for what God's prayer is. Group members are willing to stay in the presence of God on behalf of another.

Reflection Questions (based on questions developed by Shalem):

1. What was going on between you and God that made it seem right to participate in group spiritual direction this year?

2. As you recall your walk with God in these months, how has/has not group spiritual direction been a part of that walk?

3. What has been the gift? The resistance? The joy? The pain of your participation?

4. Any sense of being drawn to or away from being in a group next year?

5. Anything else?

IV.

Group Spiritual Direction in a Variety of Settings

Up to this point, we have been talking mostly about group spiritual direction in traditional religious settings, the places where one might expect to find it. But group spiritual direction, or at least a variation of it, need not be limited to these settings.

The following essays offer creative possibilities for adapting group spiritual direction to nontraditional settings. As you read at least a few of these essays, you may be saying to yourself, "What makes this group spiritual direction? It doesn't seem like what I've been reading about up to this point." And you are probably right. Not all of these essays will describe group spiritual direction in its purest sense. Yet, if you read carefully, I hope you will recognize that these groups are bearing some of the same fruits we hope will be available through group spiritual direction: People are living more authentically from their centers where they are themselves in God; they have companions who support them in their authenticity; and they are willing to be companions for others in this.

Each of the authors understands the dynamic of group spiritual direction and has felt free to adapt the process to serve the needs of those in their unique settings. What is important is not whether they are offering pure group spiritual direction but that what they are offering flows from their own sense of calling and discernment about what will best fit their groups. This is, after all, what is important in any ministry.

A word of caution is in order here. As you read these essays and reflect on appropriate adaptations for groups you are called to be with, don't be too quick to discard the heart of the process in favor of something you think might be more attractive to your clientele. People will never know the gifts of silence, prayerful listening, and spiritual community unless we invite them into these. They may see groups like those for spiritual direction as being "unproductive," and may pull away from "wasting" this time on themselves unless we issue this challenge. They may well not imagine that this "wasting time" on themselves can be for the benefit of our world unless we hold up this possibility. True, we will need to be creative in our invitational language and our adaptation of the process. We may need to move out of our comfort zones, letting go of what has worked for us in other settings so we can embrace the mystery that is beyond all methods and knowing. In fact, we may be short-changing people unless we are willing to risk offering them something counter-cultural. This can only happen as we stay close to our own centers, each step along the way.

Rose Mary Dougherty

Tending to Spirituality in the Workplace

Liz Ellmann

Group Spiritual Direction Workshop

In the spring of 2000, I attended Rose Mary Dougherty's group spiritual direction workshop at the annual Spiritual Directors International Conference. During this workshop, small groups of four or five spiritual directors were invited to practice group spiritual direction. Some participants were familiar with Rose Mary's work, and others were novices like myself. I took the workshop to learn more about how to facilitate group spiritual direction with the population I currently minister to: corporate executives.

The opening prayer set the tone for the remainder of the workshop and put group spiritual direction into a global healing context. Simply inviting us into silent reflection and then asking us to imagine someone for whom we cared deeply and for whom we might dedicate our time created the space and the time for us to "do our work for the world." These invitations were made in an unhurried, grounded way, with long, prayerful pauses that nurtured shared, large group silence. Community at the soul level was knitted together with attentiveness to the shared silence and the invitation to devote our work to a person and the world.

In the ensuing hour and a half, Rose Mary acted as timekeeper and prayerful protector of space as small groups of spiritual directors practiced the art of group spiritual direction. My group of four experienced a deep, prayerful bonding as we each shared what was bubbling up from our depths. We began each round in silence. We listened prayerfully to the heart and soul of the speaker before returning to silence. In the silence, we listened for God's response through us to what the speaker had shared. If we had something to offer the speaker, we shared God's response through us. Again, we returned to silence, giving thanks and praise for the gifts of the speaker.

Each round was brief and deep. It reminded me of the work I do with corporate executives who often do not make much time for nurturing their spirituality. Yet, given the opportunity to learn some simple centering and grounding, they are able to go deep in a short period of time. The hunger for the space and time to enter the inner depths of spirituality is palpable in organizations. Group spiritual direction is one vehicle for providing individuals an opportunity to grow spiritually and to learn how to dedicate their work for the sake of those they care most about and for our world.

The necessary ingredients for group spiritual direction are a readiness to encounter mystery; a desire to learn how to listen with ear, heart, and soul; a willingness to stay in the discomfort that can come with practicing shared silence; a thankful heart for the gift of community God has gathered for God's revelation of God's self; and a desire to learn how to reflect back and articulate what God might be revealing through us individually and as a group.

In this essay, I encourage and inspire spiritual directors to experiment with offering group spiritual direction in the workplace because:

1. We workers are hungry for experiences that invite us to recognize God in all things, even our work;
2. The structure of traditional corporate and religious institutions is undergoing radical transformation, creating feelings of fear and chaos as well as excitement and impatience;
3. The ecological and psychological limits of Western culture's propensity toward individualism and materialism are being reached; and
4. Multicultural, multi-ethnic, multi-faith workforces are inviting a reintegration and reappropriation of spirituality in work.

While group spiritual direction offers no panacea for employee retention, health care cost reduction, or ensuring peace and justice in the workplace, group spiritual direction can provide support for workers to reconnect with aspirations and focus on healthy ways of working. Tending to the spirituality of workers can offer our world the possibility of creating sustainable ways to work and live together with justice and peace.

Liz Ellmann

We yearn for safe places to ask "big questions" and to listen collectively for "big answers": "Why am I here? How am I making the world a better place?" We struggle to find meaning in organizations that we depend on for our livelihoods and that change rapidly. Group spiritual direction in the workplace offers a way and a sacred place to look for meaning by tending to the spiritual journey.

Language

I do not use the words *group spiritual direction* to invite corporate participants. Even the word *spirituality* I use sparingly in the workplace. Some may argue that what I do is not group spiritual direction at all. Yet my *intention* is to nurture a form of spirituality in a group context with the hope of building community at a soul level.

In *Presence: The Journal for Spiritual Directors International*, Felicia McKnight writes about the importance of intention and the wide variety of forms group spiritual direction takes:

> Gradually, the great "Aha" begins to dawn for those trained in spiritual direction, and then for the participants, that what they are really doing is spiritual direction at its finest. They simply have yet to name it such. The "literal" name that each group chooses will vary, depending upon the context in which the group arises. In the prophetic recognition of the internal intentionality of the group, and in the creative naming of the reality that is occurring, group spiritual

direction comes into being in one of its numberless
possibilities of form.[1]

What we do in corporate conference rooms may not be called
"group spiritual direction," yet the process generally elicits an
Aha from those trained in spiritual direction who learn about our
programs.

I am steeped in the language, study, and practice of spiritual direction. As a Roman Catholic laywoman, I earned a
Master of Divinity degree from Seattle University, a Jesuit institution. For seven years, I have practiced spiritual direction using
The Spiritual Exercises of Saint Ignatius. My education and
experience have taught me that the language of spirituality is
complex and laden with baggage. "Spirituality" and "spiritual
direction" are specialized terms rooted in historical, spiritual traditions. In order to be communicated clearly, the words *spirituality* and *spiritual direction* need to be unpacked and explained
with many nuances. *Spirituality* means one thing to a Jesuit,
another thing to a fundamentalist or New Age practitioner, and
yet another thing to a person with no religious affiliation.

A beautiful yet hidden truth lives in the diverse language
used to describe the traditional roots and historical interpretations
of spirituality. The diversity of language can also lead to ugly confusion and misinterpretation in the workplace. My partner in
ministry, Bruce Davis, M.D., is a Unitarian Universalist. We often
need to assure organizations that the goal of our group process is
not to convert participants to a particular spiritual tradition but
instead to offer tools and experiences that will aid workers—from

whatever tradition or from no tradition at all—in connecting their values and beliefs with their work. In fact, in many of our programs we do not use the term "spirituality" at all but instead use "creativity" or "innovation" as vehicles for spirituality.

My favorite definition of *spirituality* comes from Dr. Stephen Sundborg, S.J., President of Seattle University: "Spirituality is one's lived relationship with mystery." He introduced this definition of spirituality to a group of corporate executives in Seattle University's Executive Leadership Program. These executives—from a variety of religious backgrounds, and some with no religious affiliation at all—expressed appreciation for his inclusive definition. Building on Sundborg's definition, "group spiritual direction" is created by a group that intentionally listens to and looks for a lived relationship with mystery. I personally choose to name that mystery "God," but I am very cautious about using God-language in the workplace. Instead, Bruce and I encourage group participants to name mystery in whatever way they choose. We devote a whole session to exploring ways to name That Which Lives Beyond Names. During subsequent group sessions, we use the language of the participants. I invite you to substitute whatever language has meaning for you as you read this essay.

My prior experience in the corporate world and Bruce's work as a family physician and leader in a large health care organization help us translate spiritual language and values into terms understood in the corporate world. For instance, many corporate leaders want to know how their organizations might benefit from their employees being involved in group spiritual direction. We address this concern by pointing to the fact that reconnecting with and nurturing our relationship with our loving creator God frees our creative spirits. This can be an entrée for workplace spirituality programs. It may also address the skepticism of those who criticize workplace spirituality programs as a "corporate tool" to placate workers. My belief and experience indicate a different trend: Spirituality in the workplace awakens workers' deep desires and reorients work around core values that enliven and even challenge the workplace.

Writer Annie Dillard asks, "Does anyone have the foggiest idea what sort of power we so blithely invoke [when we pray]?"[2] Spirituality has the explosive potential to awaken us to unique and deeply creative work, affirming purpose and meaning beyond the paycheck. It nurtures our aliveness in all areas of life. We have witnessed transformation not only in individuals but also in organizations that attend to group spiritual direction.

Ways to Prepare for Group Spiritual Direction in the Workplace

Consider prayerfully if you are being called to this ministry, keeping in mind criticism and skepticism abound and funding is scarce. In prayer and in dialogue with your own spiritual director, ask yourself these questions:

1. What attracts me to this work?
2. What about my life journey makes me uniquely qualified to do this work?

3. Who are my allies as I explore this ministry?
4. How will I recognize confirmation of my call to this ministry?

My own discernment, experimentation, and confirmation happened over many years. When I entered divinity school, I thought I was training for ministry in a church building. However, as my education progressed and discernment deepened, I began to see ministry as a way of being in the world, not only practiced in religious buildings but ultimately everywhere. What would happen if lawyers saw themselves as ministers? Wall Street traders practiced ministry in their trades? Or computer programmers envisioned their true vocation as ministerial? These idealistic questions would not subside.

After graduating from divinity school, chaplaincy internships in hospice settings and a social analysis project at a start-up dot-com company gave me the courage to explore entrepreneurial ministry. At the dot-com company, I interviewed young workers about what gave them energy in their work and what drained them of energy. This is an Ignatian tool for the discernment of spirits. I discovered that by simply asking these questions in their work setting, some workers identified solitude as the element they needed to increase, and some began eliminating those things that deadened their daily routines. I witnessed "new birth" as a young techie recognized his power to choose. I began to recognize with increasing awareness how God has been preparing me all my life for the work I am now doing as a "hospice chaplain and midwife" in organizations that are undergoing radical transformation. After enduring much confusion during divinity school about where God was calling me (mostly because my expectation was to be working in a church building), it became clear that my spiritual direction ministry would be a ministry of presence primarily to working people in conference rooms, not church buildings.

This call has been confirmed by incredible collegial support that God has provided during the past two years through workshop cofacilitators, my ministerial partner (who truly is a godsend), Seattle University's Executive Leadership Program director, my parish, and the many participants desiring group spiritual direction in the workplace. I seek regular guidance from a spiritual director and participate in a monthly supervision group for spiritual directors. Their support and wisdom have been instrumental in the success of our workplace experiments.

Since spiritual direction is always a process of interpreting and reinterpreting words and experiences in an effort to discover how inner and outer realms relate, a spiritual director intending to facilitate workplace groups would be wise to set aside preconceived biases concerning "the evil corporate empire." Cultivating reverent curiosity may include questions that help keep personal agendas in check:

- What is God creating through this group of people?

- How is this group or organization already a manifestation of God's love?

- What blindness in me prevents me from witnessing God in this organization, in this worker, in this executive?

- What is God wanting to create in me through my work with this group?

As facilitators of workplace spirituality, we need to be respectful of how God is operating in the inner and outer realms and be honest about our motives for facilitating God's work. There may be opportunities to challenge unjust corporate systems, but if that is the personal agenda of the spiritual director-facilitator, I suggest some other venue.

To keep abreast of the newest organizational ideas and corporate lingo, I recommend reading current leadership development books and subscribing to a business magazine. (For a resource list, see www.soultenders.org.) In my role as adjunct faculty and executive coach in Seattle University's Executive Leadership Program, I also take advantage of learning from cutting-edge academic research and incorporate academic language into spiritual direction when appropriate.

Getting Started: Experimenting with Workplace Group Spiritual Direction

I am experimenting with several different venues for group spiritual direction in the workplace. Some programs use a background text. In my opinion, a textbook helps in marketing and identifying a group that is ready to do inner work, but the book is not ultimately important. In other words, the book provides a vehicle for gathering a group that yearns to learn and connect at a deeper level. As nationally recognized authors and leaders, Julia Cameron and Parker Palmer provide excellent background textbooks.

My venues include a twelve-week series, meeting for one hour (or an hour and a half if the group size is greater than ten people) during the workday in a downtown conference room. Some groups consist of people working in different industries (high tech, biotech, legal, real estate development, entrepreneur, government, education), and other groups consist of participants from the same organization. The groups are multi-faith, multi-ethnic, and multicultural. Attendance has been evenly balanced between men and women. I also have led two three-hour sessions to train people who feel called to facilitate ongoing group spiritual direction circles in their organizations; an eight-week series, meeting for one hour a week during the workday in a central university setting; and a four-week series from noon to 1 P.M. in a downtown, centrally located church classroom.

Working professionals live in a timebound world. The one-hour format during the workday fits into their timeframe. Likewise, the twelve-week series corresponds to the conventional quarter of the business cycle. The short, one-hour timeframe may seem unusual to traditional group spiritual direction, but our experience shows that participants will go deeper more quickly when given a limited amount of time. Over time, there is less and less wading and more and more deep diving where only the essential is shared and silence is welcomed instead of fought. To respect participants' schedules, we start and end on time.

Liz Ellmann

The hours of day that have been most successful are right after lunch (1:30 to 2:30 P.M.) and the cusp at the end of the workday (4:00 to 5:00 P.M.). It's generally easier to book consecutive conference room space at the end of the day, and returning to the same room each week may facilitate a deepened experience of timelessness in a time-bound group of people. Our intention is to eliminate as many distractions as possible in order to offer the group what William Blake called "Auguries of Innocence":

To see a World in a Grain of Sand
And a Heaven in a Wild Flower
Hold Infinity in the palm of your hand
And Eternity in an hour.

Participants arrive to find hospitality in the form of refreshments, name tags, and warm greetings. By using centerpieces on the conference table and wall adornments (for example, posters, charts), we create intrigue, curiosity, and a visual or sensual aid to experiencing "eternity in an hour." We do our best to transform the predictable, gray conference room with seats around a central table into an unpredictable, inviting, gathering space.

It is probably no surprise that word of mouth draws the majority of participants for these groups. Other marketing consists of circulating e-mails, blanketing downtown bulletin boards with flyers, and pleading for space in church bulletins. Being featured in *Vanity Fair* magazine and the *Seattle Times* has helped. Our SoulTenders Web site, www.soultenders.org, also announces upcoming series and events. Even if flyers and brochures do not produce many group participants, the announcements act as a downtown form of ministry by begging the question of spirituality in work.

Funding for the groups is provided by fee for service. Participants pay for the programs in the beginning, with many participants treating their workshop fee as professional development. One organization underwrote two twelve-week series and paid for us to train in-house facilitators so they could continue creating groups. They are calling their in-house group spiritual direction circles "Creativity@Work." Recently, a quickly growing high-tech organization enrolled eight people in a twelve-week series. The handpicked participants constitute a pilot group that will assess whether their organization would benefit from in-house groups.

The importance of a convenient location cannot be overstated. Downtown space for my own experiments has been God-sent. I suggest prayerfully listening to where God is leading to space availability. Law firms, brokerage houses, banks, and universities often have conference rooms in convenient downtown locations. Who in your church, synagogue, mosque, or temple might be able to offer a weekday conference room?

More Details on the Twelve-Week Series

During the course of the twelve-week series, we increase the amount of silence each session. The fidgety reaction to our first invitation to "shared silence" eventually evolves to a quieter group experience. Silence grounds the experience and cannot be overemphasized. We open and close each session with a prayerful, poetic reading, followed by shared silence and the ringing of a bell to end the shared silence.

We begin the series by instructing participants about listening, not giving advice or judging. They practice using "reflective technologies" (spiritual practices) such as stream-of-consciousness writing first thing in the morning and taking time out during the workweek to refill their creative wellspring. During the last third of the series, we borrow the prayer I learned at the group spiritual direction workshop that I wrote about earlier: "On whose behalf are you doing your work today?" This opening prayer helps orient the person toward work as a spiritual practice that can be intentionally devoted to the service of others.

Why do we do a creative expression exercise? Inviting people to create something—in this moment—offers them the experience of entering mystery. These exercises also help people talk at a deeper level; they facilitate deep sharing. Moreover, inspirational breakthroughs and reconnecting with our loving creator can be proclaimed and celebrated.

Conclusion

Some members of my parish of Saint Thérèse in Seattle call my workplace group spiritual direction "missionary work." In fact, Saint Thérèse of Lisieux is the patron saint of missionary work and has certainly guided me through a labyrinth of skeptics and critics. But workplace spirituality is not about traditional proselytizing or evangelizing. Particularly in the unchurched Northwest, there is a need for teaching spiritual language and practice by awakening individuals and the community to the spiritual journey while trusting that God will ultimately lead each person to a faith community that will help him or her continue the journey. In the language of the Roman Catholic tradition, this is pre–RCIA (Rite of Christian Initiation for Adults) work for the many who have no connections to any faith tradition. It is also pre-Judaism work, pre-Buddhist work, pre-Muslim work, pre-Protestant work, pre-Hindu work. Only God knows where each person's spirit will be best nourished. Group spiritual direction in the workplace involves gently following the lead of our creator God who longs for all people to be whole, to work and live out of our holiness, and to be secure enough to take risks for justice and peace, not only in our workplaces but also in our world.

Notes

1. Felicia B. McKnight, "Group Spiritual Direction: Intentionality and Diversity," *Presence: The Journal of Spiritual Directors International* 1, 3 (September 1995), 31.
2. Annie Dillard, "Expedition to the Pole," *Teaching a Stone to Talk* (New York: Harper and Row, 1982), 40–41.

Sacred Story, Sacred Text

Nancy Brousseau

Introduction

I began my formal studies in spiritual direction and individual retreat direction twenty years ago. My background is in the Ignatian tradition, with completion of supervised training in the *Spiritual Exercises*, directed retreat ministry, and spiritual direction practicum. My interest in group spiritual direction began several years ago as director of an adult faith development/resource center in Des Moines, Iowa.

In 1997, I was asked to become director of spiritual formation at Dominican Center, a ministry of my religious congregation. I was asked to develop a comprehensive spiritual formation program that would offer a variety of program tracks for all interested adults as well as for those seeking education and formation as spiritual directors or spiritual companions.

The ministry of spiritual formation at Dominican Center is rooted in the charism of the Dominican tradition and the Catholic Christian way of life. The Dominican motto, "To contemplate and give to others the fruit of our contemplation," grounds the Order of Preachers. The center's mission, however, is for all who seek meaning, healing, and connection in an inclusive and hospitable environment. Prayer, learning, collaboration, and hospitality guide our purpose and vision of an integrated spiritual ministry in the contemplative tradition. It is from this framework that I began to develop and expand the spiritual formation ministry and the spiritual direction programs in particular.

As I reflect on how I have come to understand group spiritual direction as a vital need in our world today and my commitment to offering it at Dominican Center, I am struck by something to which I had not previously given much thought. The process of group spiritual direction, as Shalem teaches it, resonated with my heart and soul when I began to offer workshops and other ongoing opportunities for the practice of group *lectio divina*, or what we refer to as the liturgy of *lectio divina*. The experience of *lectio* and its regular practice seems to create an "underlying spiritual rhythm." The ancient prayer form—a slow, meditative reading of scripture—interweaves word and silence within a listening, prayerful, and discerning community. The underlying rhythm begins to emerge in the individual and in the community of "spiritual friends." Gradually and gently over time, that spiritual rhythm invites participants to open their lives, their work, desires, and relationships to God and to grow in deeper awareness of God's indwelling presence, the divine Spirit already at work in their hearts.

In the Middle Ages, the Scholastic understanding of *lectio divina* was spoken of as consisting of four movements: sacred reading *(lectio)*, reflection on the scriptures *(meditatio)*, prayer response *(oratio)*, and resting in God *(contemplatio)*. In the earlier monastic tradition, the practice was thought to be circular rather than steps or stages—four moments all connected to one another and to the Spirit of God who speaks through both the sacred Word and the heart of the listener. One's prayer may begin at any of these moments, depending on the movement and drawing of the Spirit within the person praying. How strikingly similar to the process and dynamic of group spiritual direction!

Out of my own religious heritage, I began to understand the "underlying spiritual rhythm" of group spiritual direction. I came to recognize similarities in both processes. Both had a similar effect on my soul and a corresponding movement outward toward my neighbor calling me to continual integration of contemplation and action.

I developed a way of doing *lectio* in a group setting that allows for the reading of the scriptures several times aloud, silent meditation time after each reading, followed by an invitation to share. The sharing expands after each silent period, beginning first with a word, then a phrase that has touched one's heart, and finally, a sentence or two of what one has seen or heard in the silence.

The *Lectio* of Life: Sharing Sacred Story

In *lectio*, as the "reading" of one's life, what the speaker shares is indeed sacred story. The way we listen and respond to this story is often lessened in our culture by the speed with which life happens on a daily basis. Listening and speaking from the soul has become something quite rare, probably because the cultivation and art of friendship also seems less of a reality in a society where busyness and productivity appear to be of higher value. It has been helpful for me to draw on this ancient prayer form as foundational to listening and discerning God's presence within the spiritual direction group.

Forty-five individuals, many spiritual directors and social workers, participated in a weekend with Rose Mary Dougherty, and interest was sparked. As a result, five women registered for our first spiritual direction group. They were therapists, a spiritual director, teacher, nurse, and social activist, representing a variety of religious backgrounds. I served as facilitator.

There was no formal screening process for the group. For the most part, participants seemed to be compatible, given our random group arrangements. Overall it was a positive experience. Beginning each session by inviting participants to join with group *lectio* in the chapel worked well. Often, group members mentioned how the reading of the day connected with their personal prayer or spiritual journey significantly. Both processes, spiritual direction and *lectio*, seemed to support one another as the rhythm of silence and word, soul listening and soul speaking, enriched both the personal and communal aspects of their spiritual journey.

With the encouragement of staff and those first five participants, we began to advertise group spiritual direction as an offering from the Dominican Center. Consequently, we had twenty individuals in five groups for a total of nine monthly sessions. Again, evaluation continued to be positive. Our experience as facilitators was overwhelmingly encouraging. We shared amazement and awe at how quickly individuals seemed to adjust to the process and grow in silence and prayerfulness.

Group Spiritual Direction for an Underserved Population: A Collaborative Venture

In my ongoing discernment and reflection on what was happening to those involved in small groups, I began to think about opportunities for those who might not otherwise ever have such a life-giving opportunity. There are very basic reasons why this might be so: first, because they might not be able to afford it, and second, because of a lack of transportation to our center, which is located several miles from the center of the city. The executive director of Heartside Ministries, an inner-city ministry offering medical, spiritual, and physical assistance to the homeless, takes a "day away" at Dominican Center once a week. In passing, one day in the fall of 1999, I mentioned to her my hope of being able to offer spiritual direction at Heartside if we could work out the details. She was very interested. However, time passed and other programs took my attention until a beginning spiritual director in the second year of the practicum mentioned his interest in being able to do spiritual direction with the homeless. I immediately knew this was the moment. He and I invited another associate in the spiritual direction practicum who lives in the downtown area to join us in moving this dream forward.

In April 2000, Dominican Center began a collaboration with Heartside Ministries and Dwelling Place in downtown Grand Rapids to offer group spiritual direction for their primary clientele, the homeless. This relationship fulfills two of the goals of the Dominican Center's spiritual formation program: (1) to incorporate formation of group spiritual direction facilitation within the program, and (2) to extend spiritual growth offerings to all people regardless of economic or social circumstances. As a spirituality center, we believe that the group direction program offers practical ways to foster the contemplative stance of presence to God for all people from all walks of life.

In meeting with staff from Heartside Ministries, we explored all aspects of group spiritual direction and what it would take to move our plans forward, and we discussed potential obstacles and other concerns. There was serious concern about confidentiality: At Heartside, everyone knows everyone else, and not even Alcoholics Anonymous (AA) recovery groups in the Heartside district can ensure anonymity, so they are offered in other locations. Furthermore, many of the individuals seeking housing and services are in and out of recovery from drugs and alcohol and may have additional issues to be considered. This meant we would need a very intentional screening process.

Nancy Brousseau

Although in those initial conversations we assumed that we, the facilitators, would meet the participants in their locale rather than in the upscale area where the center is located, we came to see the Dominican Center as the best solution. Heartside clients who had an opportunity to attend events off-site were usually very appreciative and receptive, and the Dominican Center has a reputation for providing safe, hospitable, and inclusive space for dialogue.

We agreed that those responsible for screening would be members of our planning team already working with residents. We suggested the following criteria:

- Participants make a commitment to pray regularly;

- Participants be able and willing to share their experience of God with others;

- Participants exhibit a certain level of trust;

- Participants be able to attend the monthly sessions, regularly if at all possible.

Round-trip transportation would be provided.

As to confidentiality, I suggested that we emphasize its importance with a closing ritual at the end of each session. We decided to use a gift-wrapped box that would symbolize the gift received that day. The ribbon and bow could be removed and the top lifted off the box. Each participant would be asked to symbolically place a gift in the box. We decided to end each session with something like the following: "The gifts we received here, the gift of each person and each story as sacred story, are placed in this sacred gift box until we meet again next month. During the days ahead if we remember something of that story, something of what we heard here, we will simply hold that person in prayer as a gift to each of us." After each person held the box and "placed" in it the gift received that day, we would put the cover back on and once again tie the ribbon and bow back in place. The gift box, a candle, and a Bible were the central focus in each group gathering.

In terms of the actual process, our decision was to keep the same format as with the other groups, so each person would have fifteen minutes to share, followed by silent prayer and listening for approximately three to four minutes. Response from those in the group would last about twenty minutes, followed by silent prayer for the one presenting. Then, the next person would share, and so on.

One additional change we made was in how we would begin each session. I had spent some time at the Heartside chapel and observed that many of the people have wonderful musical ability, and they love to sing hymns. With that in mind I suggested that we begin with a sung *lectio*, a scripture-based chant, a familiar hymn, or a scripture reading and hymn that might be suitable. This would be followed by silent prayer or reflection. We agreed to schedule six sessions and an evaluation session. At that time, based on facilitator input and feedback from the Heartside/Dwelling Place staff and from participants, we would decide the next steps in this collaboration.

After weeks of conversation and preparation, we welcomed six participants to the first session, an introduction to the process and to one another. At the end of the two hours, three individuals were certain they would be back and one was very definite he would not return. He described himself as being afflicted with "mind racing" and could not focus. He was concerned that the process would be too much like group therapy, and he already had enough of that! Two men in the group were good friends and went everywhere together. They participated in Heartside events together. There would be too much insecurity if one came without the other. Tom was terribly debilitated by a life of alcohol and drugs. He described himself as no longer having a memory and said he found it difficult to follow the conversation. If Dick came back, then so would Tom.

Susan expressed a great love for God and deep searching for peace. She had thought about something like this for a long time. The idea of silence and time for prayer and sharing sounded wonderful to her. Wayne delighted in God and reading scripture. He wanted more out of life but couldn't seem to make the changes necessary. He knew this was something he would benefit from, and he is eager. Finally, there was Joseph, working hard at his recovery. He was known in his community as "the Prophet," who had a good word for everyone. Joseph knew scripture, the writings of John of the Cross, and read everything on theology and religion that he could. He was an artist whose work had been exhibited. He was quick with a smile, a word of encouragement, and occasionally drifted off to sleep due to his medication.

Four of the six returned for all of the remaining sessions. Interestingly, Tom came without Dick, much to the amazement of all of us. He claimed that he would not be able to share about himself but would love to be able to listen and pray with the group. At the September session, he shared for twenty minutes. He noted that in the past when he was upset with someone he would "curse him out." Now, he said, in his soft-spoken way, "I call on God immediately." Over the months he had been praying for his friend Dick who had gone "off the wagon." He so hoped Dick would get back into recovery. At the last session we were told that Dick was back at rehabilitation and Tom was very happy for him.

The downtown staff has commented on the change in Susan, who was known for her constant anger and impatience. She seems so much more at peace. Susan shared in the August session that she had taken time the week before to apologize for an action toward someone that came out of her impatience. She herself is noticing how she is more aware of others and the strong feelings she can have. Her prayer and dependence on God has changed considerably since she began group spiritual direction.

We have made allowances for individuals to join the group when they are ready. So, sometimes we have six, or four, or five. We find that this does not jeopardize the prayerfulness or continuity of the group, perhaps because they already know each other and very quickly grasp the process we use. They are deeply prayerful and seemingly peaceful in the silence and in the sharing. The depth of sharing, insight, and prayerfulness of the group that is gathered is evident. Their love and care for us and one another is real. They are able to offer affirmation and challenge, wisdom and truth for one another.

The sacred text of their lives is opened, and they often appear transparent in the "reading." The time of soul sharing is deeply moving. Each person, including facilitator, is blessed by the gift of group and individual discernment. Each person receives what he or she needs. Each hears what she needs to hear. Grace flows abundantly. It is in this context that we have experienced the group as spiritual director, maybe more than with other groups we facilitate. The connection is deep and true. The group seems to "sink" into the very Spirit of God at prayer in its midst. The presence is almost tangible.

When we gathered for a team evaluation, it was with great enthusiasm and gratitude that we agreed to continue the collaboration. There are others for whom group spiritual direction will be a benefit; a new session was planned, new facilitators will be trained, the original four will be back, and new participants will be welcomed. We feel blessed and privileged to be able to participate in this endeavor. And the Heartside/Dwelling Place staff has not heard of anything resembling a breach of confidentiality from participants. They have only heard encouraging and positive remarks about the overall experience.

Two significant learnings stand out from our team evaluation:

1. During the orientation session, we discovered that the Shalem video on group spiritual direction does not work well in a setting like this—the language and presentation do not speak to this particular population. If anything, it

seemed to increase the sense of separation from mainstream society that our participants were already experiencing. We found that the orientation session needs to come from the heart of the facilitator. The things that need to happen in the orientation are

- Introduce the components of silence, intercessory prayer, group discernment, but do so simply and as briefly as possible (briefly review these components at the beginning of each subsequent session).

- Allow time for participants to actually experience the components and share their experience with one another.

- Ask them to share how they pray and how they experience God in their daily life.

- Provide refreshments and build in several break times.

- Create a sense of safety—a relaxed environment with clear boundaries and structure.

2. The standard format of the process, as presented by Shalem, to our great surprise works very well in this setting. During the planning stages, we discussed whether or not to retain the process in the same format as the Shalem model or to make changes to accommodate this group. Our main concern was the amount of silence built into the process. Would the Heartside people find

this an obstacle? Would the silence deter some from returning? It was at the encouragement of one team member who works regularly with the homeless that we decided not to make any changes in the overall process except for the beginning and ending adaptations mentioned earlier.

To our amazement and delight, we found the silence to be a major source of strength and peace for the participants. More than once, they have expressed a growing love of silence. They seem to find deep peace and serenity as they engage in the prayerful silence of the group experience, something that is so difficult to find as they struggle daily with all that life seems to hand them. One group member lives in a 10-foot-by-10-foot room and hears everything going on around him. He has frequently commented on the noise of TVs and radios blaring at all hours of the day and night.

Silent intercessory prayer is a powerful new reality for most of these men and women. Simply to allow God to hold each of them in that prayerful place of loving silence as they hold one another is transforming. Wayne often sighs deeply and comments how difficult it is to find words to express what silence means to him—is this a sound of letting go in God? Our team is aware that the sensitive listening required of group members seems to be helping them discover a new depth in themselves, or perhaps is creating a new depth in each participant as each becomes more comfortable with the silence.

I am grateful for the opportunity and support I have had to be able to establish so solidly the ministry of group spiritual direction at Dominican Center in such a short time. More of the center's clientele have expressed interest in participating. It is my hope to hire a coordinator for this ministry sometime in the next few months as we continue to increase group spiritual direction opportunities at Dominican Center and at off-campus sites as well. Truly, the *lectio divina* of one's life is an experiential hearing of the Word of God. Group spiritual direction is a good *lectio* that takes place in the context of soul listening and soul speaking, intercessory prayer and discernment. It is truly a gift for the transformation of the world.

References

Hall, Thelma, R.C. *Too Deep for Words: Rediscovering Lectio Divina.* New York: Paulist Press, 1988.

Magrassi, Mariano. *Praying the Bible: An Introduction to Lectio Divina.* Collegeville, MN: Liturgical Press, 1998.

Ruffing, Janet, S.M. *Uncovering Stories of Faith: Spiritual Direction and Narrative.* New York: Paulist Press, 1989, 50.

Vicaire, Marie-Humbert, O.P. *The Genius of St. Dominic.* Nagpur, India: Dominican Publications, 1983, 14, 148.

Group Spiritual Direction with Teenagers

Patricia McCulloch

As a Roman Catholic sister, I have ministered with teenagers for some eighteen years. I have worked among the rich and the poor; in suburbs, cities, and small towns; in the United States and Venezuela. Through these experiences, I have come to know that young people possess a very strong and deep spirituality. Their difficulty lies in finding the language to express it. I think that group spiritual direction offers a process by which young people can begin to put words on what is happening in their lives.

On retreat a few years ago, I heard teenagers describe life experiences that brought me to question my own approach surrounding spirituality and prayer. Consequently, I began to listen to teens differently during subsequent retreats and prayer experiences. I heard an underlying desire to further their relationship with God. Though they did not say this directly, their language spoke of wanting something more, believing in God and yet struggling to live from that starting point. I began searching for a way to help them.

I verified my impressions with my own spiritual director and my colleagues in youth ministry. They agreed with my premise and encouraged me to pursue my search to discover a way to help the young people name what was happening inside them. From a brochure, I contacted Shalem and participated in a group spiritual direction workshop. I thought the process seemed a good fit for teenagers. Young people like to be with each other. They like talking about what is happening in life, and they respond to each other's stories. Group spiritual direction offers a framework for them to share but also to listen in a different way, to hear the workings of the Spirit in each other's lives.

In this essay I describe how I used and adapted group spiritual direction with teenagers, from the criteria for invitation and a do-able way of inviting to the more spiritual components of prayer and graced moments. My hope is that this reflection will lead the reader to a deeper appreciation of the spirituality of teenagers and to discover a new way to help young people name their deepest desire—a relationship with God.

Setting and Description

As I mentioned earlier, I have ministered in many different settings. However, for the sake of simplicity, I will use one group as an example. This group was composed of high school seniors who attended the same parish church. Some attended Catholic high schools, others went to the neighboring public schools, and a few went to local private schools. All were involved in their parish youth ministry program—serving as peer ministers, participating in service opportunities, and attending retreats.

Yet these were very typical teenagers. They were not saints, and they struggled with their humanness. They each had a story. Some of them had experiences with the courts and/or the discipline boards at their schools; some just got caught by their parents. Some of them continued to live on the edge while others were the epitome of the ideal. They played sports, worked on yearbooks, held down jobs, participated in student council, and played hard on weekends. They were just teenagers trying to make sense of their world. And in this group they began to develop the skills of quieting themselves, expressing what was happening inside, and listening critically to each other.

Process of Invitation

Prior to inviting I set some criteria, based on what I knew of group spiritual direction and teens. The young people, for instance, needed to demonstrate a willingness to risk, be open, listen, sit in small amounts of silence, and be comfortable with God-talk. They needed the ability to name God in their lives or at least be able to struggle in order to put words around it. Likewise, there had to be some interest in deepening their spiritual life. One way or another, the ones I invited all expressed an interest in "something more." Because I knew the young people through working and ministering among them, I knew which ones were searching for something a little more challenging.

I think it is important to know the young people who are invited, because group spiritual direction is not for everybody. As with adult groups, there is a screening process. However, prior to inviting any potential participants, I tested them out with people who knew them because of the self-esteem issues surrounding the teenage years. Some people could benefit from group spiritual direction, and other young people needed something else.

I began the process of invitation with prayer. In the silence of my heart, I asked only to be available to God for the young people. I asked that I remain open to whomever God wanted to be a part of this process. I placed the names before God. I went into the process of invitation knowing that it was not I who called. God was in charge.

I sent a postcard to each of the potential participants. It's a good way to communicate with young people because they just flip it around and read it. In this case, nine out of ten times, a parent read the postcard and pursued it with their child. The young people's sincerity was authentic, but their planning skills were still shaky. On the postcard I simply wrote, "Looking for something more in your life? Making big decisions surrounding college? Want a way to think and pray through this year with friends? Group spiritual direction may be for you." Then I added the place, time, and how to contact me if interested.

I followed up the postcard with a phone call, believing that direct contact is best. Even though I had written on the postcard to call, they typically forgot. By phoning, I could talk with them about group spiritual direction, what the expectations included, and when we would meet. Often they committed right then and

Patricia McCulloch

there; however, I usually made a reminder call the day before our gathering.

The expectations were straightforward: they needed to commit to the process and to the group. The key elements included showing up, showing up on time, participating during the group, and praying for each other outside of the group. Likewise, the commitment to one's own spiritual life was essential. I made it clear that spiritual growth came with some work on their part. This was not a once-a-month prayer group or a free-for-all. Our time would be structured. This was about finding God in the everyday. They promised to the best of their ability.

It took a lot of explaining and inviting to get the first group started. However, after the first year it became easier. Those who came knew what to expect from the experiences of those who went before.

Experiences of Adaptation and Growth

I want to highlight a few adaptations and growth experiences that may help the reader in his or her own ministry with young people. First, I tried to adapt the process while keeping its integrity. This was a challenge. Some of the language used for adults does not translate well for seventeen-year-olds. For instance, the words *intercessory prayer* meant nothing to them (I explain later in detail how I adapted this key concept). Even though the young people were to a certain degree comfortable with silence and stillness, the amount of time and how it was

202

used within group spiritual direction remained challenging. Consequently, I adapted.

We began slowly. The young people often came from practices, homework, or jobs. As we all know, teens are social beings. They love to talk to each other. Consequently, I always gave them ten minutes to catch up with one another and eat. Yes, I provided food—always soda and some variety of junk food. It helped them settle down.

We gathered in a space different from where we socialized. The room was set up in such a way that it told them, through their senses, that something different was happening. For instance, the overhead light was out and candles were everywhere; instrumental music played and pillows were on the floor. They entered the room and settled into the space. They simply relaxed. The atmosphere was comfortable and safe. They knew that they could be themselves and say what was on their minds as they entered into this place that became very, very special.

We always began with my reminder of why we gathered—to be available to God for each other. I started our time together giving the group to God and drawing everybody into the circle of light. I would say something like:

> God is here amongst us.
> God is right here at the center of our circle.
> This is our time with God.
> Let us spend some time just looking back over our
>   days since the last time we gathered. Where was
>   God?

Where was God seemingly missing?

As you look at your life, where do you desire God?

As you pray and review, be attentive to what keeps rising up.

If you keep coming back to a certain experience or desire, just sit with it and ask God to show you whatever it is you are to see.

After shaping the quiet time, I invited them to get comfortable—they stretched out, curled up on the floor—however they wanted. Once they settled, I reminded them not to move around too much, as they might become a distraction for others. For some of the young people, they needed the discipline of writing in order to stay focused. Others read their journals, while some just lay there.

As I called them together, I reviewed the process. One person shared what came forth in her prayer. The rest of us prayed with and for this person as we listened. I stressed that the trick in all of this was not to get captured into their own stories. Upon hearing someone's story, it is so very easy for our minds to respond, react, retell. Everyone worked hard to stay present to the person sharing. I offered them the mantra: "Help me be available to you, God, for this person."

I was the timekeeper, and I worked diligently to keep the young people on task. Because they took direction at school, they handled it with only gentle reminders. At the two-minute mark, for example, I gave the person sharing a sign and again at thirty seconds. Throughout the process, in order to keep them on task,

I named the next step. I found that they did better with a step-by-step explanation rather than setting out the entire framework at the beginning. Naturally, at our first gathering I explained the entire process; however, at our monthly sessions I just did it as we went along.

Although keeping them on task as we went along helped, I closely monitored their responses. As I said before, they typically got caught in telling their own stories, reacting and comparing, taking the experience quickly into conversation. It took them a while to learn the skill of responding from that place inside of them that heard and listened to the person sharing. I finally found that the following explanation helped: "Before you share, check in with yourself and make sure it is of God; if it keeps coming back, then trust yourself and tell us. However, if it is just a comment that you want to share, then you may want to wait for later in order not to take the process into a conversation."

As the young people became comfortable with the process and felt safe with each other and me, they opened up. Naturally, this is one of the points behind group spiritual direction. However, it took energy for me to sit there and not react. For example, some young people shared about times around drinking, and that was hard enough, but add in drinking and driving, drinking and drugs, drinking and sex. I began questioning the process and myself. Was I doing the right thing? What should I say? Do? Maybe they are too young for this? I gave them to God when they shared and again asked God to help me be available. I learned to trust in a new way.

Since I played the role of facilitator and not participant, I chose not to share readily. Even though in adult groups the facilitator participates in the response to sharing, I am of the philosophy that when adults insert thoughts and comments it typically causes young people to stop talking. I found that this group took care of it for me. God worked through them amazingly well.

One young person shared that she no longer knew if God really existed. She talked about this for some time. It did not make sense, because this young lady usually talked freely about God and God's love. Throughout her high school days she embodied a strong faith. I sat there, being timekeeper, praying hard but still getting caught in a mild panic that she might be having a crisis of faith. When the time came to respond, one of the boys asked, "So what are you doing that you know you aren't supposed to be?" I was shocked. I thought that he had totally not heard the story. However, I was the one who missed it. Through their language, the young lady communicated that she was partying and loving it. She thought that to be faithful one could not party; therefore, she started pulling back from God. As the group directed, shared, listened, and prayed, they struggled to find God in their social life. Through it all, I just kept praying and watching the time.

Sometimes during group sharing, they asked me what I thought. I told them that my opinion was not the point of group spiritual direction and that we needed to sit in prayer. This shocked them. They often gave me enough information to point out so many things. However, they knew this already. They knew right from wrong. By my staying firm and rooted in the process,

I allowed God to work and I got out of the way. During the evening, as the sharing of stories took place and the prayer deepened, they came to a place of recognizing God's gentle nudge to straighten the path.

Don't get me wrong—when these sessions were over, they usually asked again what I thought and I readily obliged if it had to do with such important subjects as drinking and driving. Sometimes they asked as a group. Other times a young person stayed back and waited for everyone else to leave. Something had been sparked within the person and he or she needed some one-on-one time. Their intensity was very real. As with so many in their age group, these teenagers felt things deeply and they needed someone to listen to them. I found group spiritual direction triggered some of these deep emotions. Personally, I thought it invaluable to be available to them as they discerned what God said in the midst of the confusion around them.

This was very different from the adult group I facilitated. As would be expected, the adult group was self-directed. We considered ourselves peers. This was not true in my teenaged group, because I, the facilitator, was an adult. I was an authority to the teenagers and at times looked to for guidance. Therefore, when a young person asked to talk, I tried to keep the atmosphere reflective as if we were in spiritual direction. I resisted offering my opinion, choosing to continue to pray while I listened. I asked questions in such a way that enabled the young person to discern God's call in the midst of the struggle. Although I did not expect or seek out these conversations, upon reflection, I think their occurrences were only natural. Once one begins to open up and feel the Spirit's touch, it brings to the surface many different thoughts and emotions. Unlike the facilitator of adult groups, the adult offering group spiritual direction to teenagers must be available and capable to walk with the young people on their individual journeys as well.

Prayer

One of the most exciting parts of group spiritual direction was the prayer component. Prior to participating in the group, the young people committed to prayer, not only for themselves but also for the world and each other. Typically, I found it easy for young people to see the value of praying, and they did it readily whenever they gathered for prayer. However, it took self-discipline to make prayer a daily practice. I maintained the high expectation that they develop this life skill that they would draw on for years to come.

I never used the words *intercessory prayer*, and I did not explain it as taught at the group spiritual direction workshop. Instead, I interpreted the concept and described it in terminology understood by the young people without losing the essence of this prayer style. I invited them to sit and allow their minds to be a PowerPoint presentation, viewing all the different pictures of places and people in the world that needed God's love. From this, I invited them to ask God to reveal one situation that needed their prayer, their full attention.

During the group, after people shared, they told us how to specifically pray for them during the next month. I found this a powerful time. I originally did this piece at the end; however, the sacredness of their specific moment of sharing seemed lost. It worked better with the teenagers to do it after a person spoke. At the end, as part of our closing prayer, I reminded everyone of each person's prayer intentions and called them back into our circle of light once again.

By promising to pray for each other, I hoped that the discipline of a practice of daily prayer and silence would become a part of their lives. Even though I never knew for sure, I saw growth in their readiness to speak and the depth of their sharing. Our time together went deep very quickly. I saw a change in how they prayed, not only during the group but when they gathered with the larger youth community.

Support

Without a doubt, support for me remained critical. In the beginning, I touched base with a Shalem mentor. I found it helpful to talk to someone who kept before me the integrity of group spiritual direction. We talked a lot about balancing the process with the developmental level of teenagers. As I struggled, for example, with whether or not to use music, my mentor reminded me of the importance of silence. Subsequently, I began to encourage young people to grow more and more comfortable with silence. The most fascinating thing occurred—the teenagers themselves eventually found the music distracting and turned it off! They, too, came to desire silence.

I also felt the prayer support of people around me. I never went into the group alone. I truly believed that other people held me in prayer and would help me step back and not control, to allow the Spirit free reign. I was to stay available to God for the group.

My own spiritual director greatly supported me. I leaned on her greatly during the beginning months. I would not recommend facilitating a group of teenagers if you are not in a group or individual spiritual direction yourself. So often I got "kidnapped" into the conversations. So often I questioned my role and myself. So often I played God. My spiritual director reminded me of who ultimately was in charge. She always asked me where God had been during the session, had I checked in with God before responding, and had I stayed true to the process. During the months that the group met, my prayer life seemed terrific. It was amazing how disciplined I became, knowing that I needed God in such a different way. It was a priority to stay grounded in my own prayer life.

Learnings

I learned so much about young people and myself during this experience. Some practical things included group size. Unfortunately, I allowed the teenagers to talk me into keeping them together. Therefore, we had about eight to ten people in one group, with four of them able to share when we gathered. They loved being together. They became a great support for one another. However, the group was too big; I would not do that again.

I think that they did pray for each other, that they looked for God in their lives, and that their hearts were in the right place. However, it might have been good to have given them concrete tools by which to encourage their own personal prayer practice—for example, a way to examine their day before going to sleep or scripture passages to read and meditate on.

Setting monthly meetings remained key. These teenagers worked from a calendar. They promised not to schedule anything else at this time. Subsequently, they negotiated their other commitments in advance.

Learning the language of the teens, when it came to expressing God's activity in their life, took time. With an understanding of spirituality and human development, I began to hear the similarities and came to appreciate better how God worked in their lives.

Letting God be God was the best learning of all! I learned more and more about how I subtly inserted my will and ignored the Spirit. By staying true to my prayer life, the rest took care of itself.

Conclusion: Grace Moments

As I reflect back on this group, the grace moments overwhelm me. The young people sincerely struggled to stay true to the process. They loved group spiritual direction; it met a need in their lives. As seniors in high school, they were in the midst of making college plans and experiencing blossoming social lives. They juggled a lot for seventeen-year-olds. Quieting down and listening to where God was leading them became central to their discernment process. For me, it was a humbling experience to be a part of it. To hear their stories as they searched for truth helped me in my own life. I could not deny the hard work and discipline that my own journey demanded. Watching the young people made me reflect on my own spiritual life.

They took their commitment seriously. They found that the group fed them in a way that nothing else did. They felt safe to say what was on their mind and knew that what they heard remained rooted in the Spirit. Their trust level truly spoke volumes. God worked through each one of them and in the group as a whole. None of us doubted it. It truly was a grace moment to see God at work.

The greatest grace, however, was the personal relationship each one developed with God. As they moved on, each could speak comfortably about that journey. Each could name what so many of us long for—a desire for an ongoing relationship with God.

I was truly graced to walk this journey with these teenagers. We cried, laughed, talked seriously, and just sat in silence with one another. They helped me take seriously their spiritual lives and taught me their language. They trusted me to hold them gently while they learned to fly on their own. Now when they come back into my life for coffee or dinner, the conversation always gets around to "How is your prayer life?" It is a natural part of our relationship.

I look at teenagers very differently since that first group. I hear things I never heard before; I ask questions that are more pointed. It does not take me long to ask about their prayer life or where they desire God. Because of my experience with group spiritual direction, I recognize the obscure openings in a conversation that a young person provides, and I readily take them. It always brings me to a new place where God and teenager meet.

Group Spiritual Direction in Seminary

A. J. van den Blink

How I Came to Teach a Course
in Group Spiritual Direction

My experience with theological education, both as a student in the 1960s and later as a faculty member at two seminaries, is that there is more talk *about* God than reflection on experiences *of* God. The same can be said, of course, about what goes on in many churches. But in seminaries, whose very purpose it is to prepare men and women for ministry, this objectification of faith without sufficient attention to the need to be grounded in the holy is, in the eyes of many, becoming increasingly problematic. As one New Testament scholar recently observed, "Learning *about* religion, theology, or spirituality may strengthen one's [sense of religious vocation], but it cannot substitute for the primary knowledge gleaned from one's own experience of the Holy."[1]

The judgment that there is something important missing at the heart of mainline theological education is a rather recent phenomenon and does not yet appear to be a majority opinion. It is true that, due to the great interest in spirituality in our culture, many seminaries are adding courses in Christian spirituality to their curricula and even founding special institutions for that purpose. Such courses are commonly located in departments of ministry or pastoral theology, but they are seldom integrated into the whole seminary curriculum. There is still a deep-seated distrust of mixing matters of mind with things of the spirit. The words of one seminary professor accurately represent, in my experience, the feelings of many faculty members: "Just as the classroom is not the place to learn to drive a car, it is similarly not the place to learn how to pray."[2] Even those who have come to favor providing some form of spiritual formation in seminaries usually envision that being done outside the classroom.

A major, but often unacknowledged, contributing factor is the radical change that has taken place in theological education over the past two centuries. Under the pervasive influence of the Enlightenment and the rise of modern science, seminaries have moved away from offering theological and spiritual formation in the tradition of their founding denominations to becoming more and more centers for the academic study of religion. In the West, this process of change began in the early 1800s with the reform of theological education in Berlin and has since spread all over Western Europe and North America.[3]

A direct consequence of this historical development has been to regard prayer and spiritual formation as the responsibility

215

of individual students and faculty members and their own denominations or religious groups. Spiritual formation came to be seen as incidental to the real work of theological education, namely that of intellectual formation. The result has been a widening gap, even in denominational seminaries, between theology and the practice of ministry, between prayer and action, between seminary and parish, and also between academic and spiritual formation.

It was not until the late 1980s, when a spiritual crisis occurred in my own life while I was already teaching in seminary, that I became more aware of this divide between the academic and the spiritual. My eyes also were opened at that time to the lack of any plan, or even intent for that matter, to help seminary students with their own spiritual formation. My own search for a more integrated spirituality led me to seek spiritual direction, to apply some time later for training at the Shalem Institute for Spiritual Formation,[4] and not long thereafter, with considerable hesitation, to offer an introductory course in spirituality which I called "Seeking God: The Way of the Spirit."[5] My hesitation was due in part to not being certain how much interest there would be in such a course. I need not have worried.

This Seeking God course functioned as a testing ground for conducting an action/reflection seminar in spiritual formation in an academic setting. The term "action/reflection" means that students not only listen to lectures on spiritual formation but practice contemplative prayer, share spiritual journeys, keep a journal, and write a paper on their own spiritual journey. Every class session begins with a brief opening prayer and ten minutes of contemplative silence, and ends with silence and closing prayers. Students practice prayerful listening to each other in the large group and in small spiritual reflection groups,[6] using a protocol that is adapted from the one developed at Shalem. Since few students in the setting where I teach are familiar with contemplative silence, with going on retreats, or for that matter, with being silent for any length of time at all, I also devote one whole class session to what I call a mini-retreat, complete with two brief retreat addresses and the observance of silence throughout.[7]

What happened in the Seeking God course was enormously encouraging. The course evaluation of one student summarizes the comments of many:

> The class was a blessing to me, truly a "God-thing." Part of me mourns its loss; but I am comforted by the fact that what took place over the past quarter is not dependent upon course offerings. The class was not, after all, about academics or learning to be a "better' Christian. The course was, I think, about relationship, community, and prayer. It was about storytelling and finding a part of our own story in the stories of others. It was, as the title said, about seeking God and the ways the Spirit helps us do just that.[8]

This introductory course provided compelling, anecdotal evidence that people from widely varying backgrounds—in terms of race, gender, denomination, and sexual preference— can make a connection on a deeper level than the usual attempts

A. J. van den Blink

at ecumenicity with which I was familiar. It also became evident that contemplative silence and the prayer to which it gives rise are able to generate the kind of Christian community that is often talked about in seminaries but seldom seen in practice. It has never ceased to amaze me how this coming together in the Spirit not only joins people to one another but affirms them in their own particularity. All this helped me trust that group spiritual direction not only *could* be done in a seminary setting but also *needed* to be done.

The Course in Group Spiritual Direction[9]

The experiences in the Seeking God course strengthened my conviction that what is needed is a reversal of the way theological education is usually done. Spiritual formation of students *and* faculty cannot be an add-on but needs to be the matrix in which and out of which *all* Christian theology and theological reflection needs to be done. Theological education needs to be done by men and women of prayer—faculty and students alike—in the context of a community of prayer.[10] I began to see that group spiritual direction can make a small but important contribution to the spiritual formation of students who are studying for the ministry or priesthood.

Design

For a sense of how I framed and managed this course as part of education for ministry, I will give a description of the course, say something about prerequisites for admission, provide a brief sketch of procedures and requirements, and describe the schedule of a typical session.

Course Description. In the syllabus I explain the reason for offering this course:

> With the rebirth of interest in Christian spirituality has come the rediscovery of the importance of spiritual guidance in the life of the believer. Providing individual spiritual direction to members of their churches, however, is usually not very practical for clergy, even if they are experienced spiritual directors, because of the time it may take to accommodate all those who are interested. Those who do one-on-one spiritual direction are also more vulnerable to problems of psychological transference and interpersonal boundaries that can arise in long-term pastoral relationships. For reasons like these, the relevance of group spiritual in the parish and in the local congregation, as well as institutional settings, is becoming increasingly evident.
>
> By far the most important rationale for making group spiritual direction available, however, is a theological one. To be a Christian is never a solitary endeavor but always involves participating in the community of believers, the Body of Christ. Providing group spiritual direction has the potential of helping people experience, often for the first time, what Christian community can be like. Group spiritual

219

direction can renew the prayer life of the faithful,
help them with their spiritual journeys, ground them
in their faith and give them a sense of the wider
Christian koinonia.[11]

With this description, I make clear that engaging in group spiritual direction is not only for the purpose of one's own spiritual
formation but also for the sake of preparing for a more grounded
and relevant ministry.

Prerequisites. The experience in the Seeking God course
taught me that many students need to have a period of preparation before they can participate fully in group spiritual direction and before they can learn something about doing group
spiritual direction in their own places of ministry. For that reason, I made the Seeking God course, or its equivalent, a prerequisite for those who wanted to sign up for Group Spiritual
Direction. By allowing the possibility of an equivalent I am
able to admit students, or clergy, who are interested in group
spiritual direction but who have not yet taken the introductory
course. I make it a practice to interview people I do not know
in order to get a sense of their readiness for group spiritual
direction. The seminary's two-week drop-add period in the
beginning of the semester affords an additional opportunity for
screening. Several times I suggested that a student withdraw
and consider taking the course later after more experience with
contemplative silence and prayerful listening.

Procedures and Requirements. Students are informed that
by taking this course they covenant to participate as actively and

honestly as they can; be willing to attend both parts of *all* class sessions, unless there is a clear emergency that prevents them from doing so; take responsibility for reading 75 to 100 pages a week without being checked up on; keep a private journal for themselves; and keep what is said and experienced in class confidential.

The work of this course is done in large and small groups. The small groups are intended to function as peer spiritual direction groups or SDGs. These SDGs are asked to follow the Shalem Protocol for Spiritual Direction Groups,[12] electing a convener on a rotating basis to be in charge of keeping time and ensuring that members stay focused on the task of discerning God's presence and direction, and refraining from socializing, problem solving, and psychological or theological analysis. I point out that, in contrast to conveners, facilitators are trusted outsiders who do not participate as members of the group but who have had experience with group spiritual direction.

Since regular attendance and the willingness to participate fully during every class session is so critical to the work of group spiritual direction, I advise students to drop this course if they already know that they will have to miss more than two sessions, are counting on being able to skip class at the end of the semester to prepare for an examination or finish a term paper—a common practice in academia—or discover, after attending a few times, that they are at a point in their life or spiritual journey where they have difficulty benefiting from a course like this.

Unlike in the Seeking God course, there are required readings (class bibliography is included as the Appendix of this essay). I tell the students that with the exception of Rose Mary

Dougherty's *Group Spiritual Direction*, which I want them to read first, it does not matter to me in what order they study the books listed. Except for two of the books where I suggest they browse around, I indicate the parts of each book that I want them to read. I explain that they are not limited to the list of required reading and that they may encounter other books that they will find useful. I ask them to share anything that they have found helpful.

I explain that their course grade will be determined by their class participation (50 percent) and their term paper (50 percent), which is intended to be a vehicle for critical reflection on their experience with group spiritual direction—either in class and/or a time-limited spiritual direction group in their field work or place of ministry. I make clear that their spirituality will not be graded, either in written or oral form, and that each student who attends regularly and takes part actively will receive an A for class participation.

I also tell them that our accountability as students and faculty members requires that educational standards be observed. I explain that their papers will, therefore, also be evaluated from an academic perspective of four criteria: clarity of expression and organization, critical use of readings and theory, quality of analysis, and use of self. I assure them that the contents of their term papers are held in strictest confidence and that they will receive a written response from me to their papers.

Schedule. Each class is organized into two periods with a break in between. The first session (75 minutes) begins with centering, opening prayer, and contemplative silence (15 minutes), is followed by a lecture by me or by a visiting colleague, and is concluded with a discussion (60 minutes). Following the break, the second session (also 75 minutes) begins with the whole group gathering for silence (5 minutes), continues with students going to their own small spiritual direction groups (55 minutes), and ends with everyone reconvening for a final feedback round and closing prayers (15 minutes).

And finally, in this course I also devote one whole class session to a mini-retreat. Since the course thus far has been offered during the spring semester, I try to schedule this retreat right before or during Holy Week and organize the two brief retreat addresses around themes of the Triduum.[13]

Issues

Academic Integrity. The issue of how to maintain academic integrity while staying away from judging the narrative, written, or oral quality of anyone's spiritual experience is one that I have given much thought to, especially given the prevailing attitude in the theological academy. I have already described my solution,[14] which appears to be working well. At another seminary where I have taught this course, the Pass/Fail grading system obviates the necessity for giving letter grades. Whatever the grading system used, I try to model academic accountability through the kind of requirements I have already described and by taking my part seriously by means of extensive written feedback to term papers.

A. J. van den Blink

Introducing Group Spiritual Direction. This is not an easy issue, given the time constraints of a course that meets once a week for two and a half hours during a thirteen-week semester or a ten-week quarter. I have tried several things to bring students up to speed. First, I assume that even those who have taken the Seeking God course need a refresher in contemplative listening. For that reason, I have them convene in spiritual reflection groups for the first few weeks of the semester, until the drop-add period is over. This also gives me the opportunity to observe people in action and screen them out if necessary.

Second, to give students a sense of group spiritual direction in action, I have tried various methods. I have shown the Shalem *Group Spiritual Direction* video; I have facilitated a small group of volunteers in front of the other students; I have facilitated a group of conveners, if the class is large enough to have more than three small groups; and I have facilitated several groups at once by keeping them together in one room for one session. The response from students, to my surprise, has been that seeing a session of group spiritual direction demonstrated *in vivo,* using any of the approaches I just outlined, is more helpful to them than only watching the videotape.

Forming Spiritual Direction Groups. I do not myself divide the students into spiritual direction groups. When the time comes for groups that will stay together for the remainder of the semester, I ask them to form into their own groups of four or five. I *do* tell them, and this is important, to avoid getting together with friends and team up instead with classmates with whom they are least familiar. This has worked well. The only time I

224

intervene is when I notice a conflict of interest. For instance, recently I discovered—fortunately before the groups got started—that one member of a group was in a position of authority over another one in their denomination.

Size of Class. The largest group of students that has taken this course thus far has numbered twenty, and the smallest eight. With the twenty students, there were five groups of four each. With eight students, there were two groups of four. My best experience to date has been with the group of eight. In retrospect this had much to do with the opportunity a smaller group affords to connect more meaningfully with each other, not only in the small group but in the large one as well. I have found that the large group is as important as the small groups, for it represents the wider Christian community and helps guard against an insularity that can develop in spiritual direction groups when there is insufficient contact with others. When things go well, there is a choreography to this course, a rhythmic flow among large group, small group, and self.

Feedback

I have divided the feedback into three categories: personal responses, general observations, and suggestions for improvement. All quotes are used with permission or are taken from course evaluations.

Personal Responses. Course evaluation[15] responses often refer to having experienced a degree of personal transformation. Here is a typical comment: "When I started seminary I not only felt that I did not know how to pray, I was afraid to pray. Spiritual direction and the added dimension of community in group spiritual direction has opened the door to a greater understanding of God, others, and myself." For some there has been the clarification of their vocation: "Experiencing group spiritual direction has been like coming home. I believe that it has given me a direction in ministry because my gifts are deeply rooted in this kind of work." Others spoke of a widening of spiritual horizons: "This course was like the Jesus Prayer—every part of it kept calling me into God's presence from a variety of different entrance ways."

Several mentioned a sense of liberation, as in this comment: "Personally...participating in this class has helped me move from a time of fear in my own life to more of a calm that is looking for God's direction. This course has helped me shed 'garbage' from my life." A common response had to do with having experienced the gift of true Christian community: "I can honestly say that for the first time in my life I experienced what it means to be a part of a *true* ecumenical community." And appreciating the gift of diversity: "The class's rich diversity was a particular joy and blessing....I appreciated your ease with affirming the feminist, Black, Protestant, Catholic, [and] Anglican perspectives and [clarifying] push-buttons, which can separate as well as enrich."

General Observations. These observations dealt with a range of topics. There was unanimous appreciation of having been exposed to the riches of contemplative prayer. "Opening with contemplative prayer was especially meaningful," one person remarked, and another added, "I simply longed for the silence and to be prayerfully present." Yet another, speaking of contemplative prayer commented: "The important factors of surrendering and submitting oneself to the Holy, over and against the influences that impinge against God, has become more evident." Journaling and the mini-retreat also were appreciated: "Keeping a journal was an excellent exercise and added deeply to the whole experience for me. The [mini] retreat was very helpful — thanks for [the copy of] your notes so I didn't have to stay in the reporter mode as I was noting the process as well as the content."

Appreciation was expressed for appropriate self-disclosure on the part of the leader: "Your comments on your own journey and how different factors of personality, culture, etc. [influence our behavior and perceptions] helped me better identify factors that get in the way and help with my own awareness of the Holy." And very important, there were comments on the critical importance of the protocol, often after initial resistance: "The protocol, which at first seemed forced, gradually became essential and became an excellent structure for the groups." Someone else wrote, "At first I didn't appreciate the structure [of the protocol] because I preferred the 'flow' of the Spirit. Using the protocol is a wonderful discipline because I now see/know how it helps me remain focused on listening for the Spirit. The discipline used within the group has made this type of prayer safe and loving." Added another, "The protocol allows one to put into practice a practical theology....I have learned to surrender into and trust the process and learned to implement it in my ministry setting."

Suggestions. Some students wanted more. "I wish we could have discussed more of the current interest in spirituality, both 'New Age' and traditional. What does it mean?" One wrote, "Please don't change anything," but then added, referring to a decision a few weeks into the course to spend the first fifteen minutes of each class session getting connected with one another, "I'm glad we added the schmooze element," and then suggested as a way for the large group to get connected, "have each student bring to the second session something meaningful in his/her life and be willing to share its meaning with the large group." Referring to the mini-retreat, the suggestion was made that "the retreat might be held in a place where there is less interruption." Several students in their enthusiasm wanted the course to be made a requirement. Others spoke of the need for an integration of this kind of spiritual formation into the seminary curriculum.

Concluding Comments

This course began as an attempt to do actual group spiritual direction within the context of an academic course. I have by now offered the course enough times to be able to say that the experiment has succeeded. My experience with this course challenges the accepted wisdom that the only way in which spiritual formation in seminary can happen is through *a complementary relationship between the classroom and its formal agenda and the program of spiritual formation that complements the classroom*[16] — in other words, by keeping a safe distance between the two. I hasten to add that spiritual formation can happen through means other than courses in spirituality, such as the one in group spiritual direction. As a matter of fact, the entire seminary experience can play an important part in one's spiritual formation. It is the privileging of academic inquiry and formation over that of spiritual formation that is the issue—as well as the fear that by not keeping a sharp boundary between the two, academic rigor will be diminished. In my experience, the opposite is true. Some of the best papers I have read have come out of this course. Also, courses in spiritual formation, such as group spiritual direction, and the deeper grounding in self, others, and God that they make possible, can make students more available to the abstract truth of theological discourse. Coming to experience the lived truth of the faith in their everyday lives can foster in students, and faculty members for that matter, a receptivity to theologies from the past and present that attempt to articulate this truth. It goes without saying that both theological and spiritual grounding are needed if the former is not to become disconnected and the latter to become rudderless.

Whether courses in group spiritual direction are offered in seminaries as academic courses or complementary experiences in spiritual formation is not as important as the availability of faculty to teach them—seminary teachers who are themselves spiritually grounded and trained in spiritual direction and who have an appreciation of the critical importance of spiritual formation in theological education. There is a powerful gyroscopic effect to the way educational systems will co-opt attempts at reform, including spiritual formation, into the curriculum. One way this manifests itself is by delegating the task of spiritual formation to one person or department and then marginalizing that person or division by assigning them to a lower, less important rung on the seminary hierarchy.

If spiritual formation is indeed central to theological education and not an add-on, then *everything* that is done in a seminary needs to be understood as playing its part in the overall formation of students, faculty, administration, and support staff. Authentic Christian spirituality is always inclusive and always communal. Spirituality in theological education cannot be the property or responsibility of any particular group, whether ordained or lay, whether theologically educated or not, whether spiritual beginners or advanced contemplatives. For that same reason, the responsibility of spiritual formation in the seminary cannot be relegated to a few who have made spirituality their particular area of expertise. It is the responsibility of everyone, and most particularly, the entire faculty.[17]

When it comes to integrating spiritual formation into the seminary curriculum, the reformation of theological education has just begun. If this change is going to be more than a repackaging of the old ways of doing things, it is going to take a while before there is a consensus about the central place of spiritual formation in theological education. Meanwhile, courses in spiritual formation, such as the one in group spiritual direction that I have described, can do their small part to enlarge the number of students and interested faculty who have been exposed to their transformative potential.

Notes

1. L. William Countryman, *Living on the Border of the Holy: Renewing the Priesthood of All* (Harrisburg, PA: Morehouse, 1999).
2. Gordon T. Smith, "Spiritual Formation in the Academy: A Unifying Model," *Theological Education* 33, 1 (1996), 86.
3. Cf. David H. Kelsey, *Between Athens and Berlin: The Theological Education Debate* (Grand Rapids: Eerdmans, 1993).
4. Shalem's Spiritual Guidance Program, Class of 1995 (Summer).
5. APT 322. The acronym APT stands for Ascetical and Pastoral Theology. I chose the title of this course to convey that seeking God *is* the way of the human spirit *as well as* the way of the Holy Spirit that resides in all of us.
6. A spiritual *reflection* group, composed of four or five students, differs from a spiritual *direction* group in that it has a broader and more focused agenda, such as practicing particular skills of prayerful listening to self, other, and God, considering particular issues that have arisen or sharing one's thoughts on questions that have been suggested for prayerful reflection.
7. During these mini-retreats students are invited, following opening contemplative silence, to go outside the classroom to find a space where they can be by themselves. The library and chapel are favorite places. Once the mini-retreat begins, they are asked to reconvene only for the retreat addresses and final prayers. I explain that observing silence need not be interpreted legalistically; that it is all right, for instance, to greet friends and colleagues whom they pass in the hallways, but I do ask them not to get involved in an ongoing conversation. To free them from having to take notes, I give them a copy of my remarks afterward. During one of these mini-retreats a students brought badges for everyone with the inscription: *In Contemplation!*
8. Private communication, used with permission.
9. APT 623 Group Spiritual Direction, Bexley Hall Seminary.

10. In the last few years, the restructured curriculum of Bexley Hall Seminary, the small Episcopal theological school where I now teach, has shown that it is possible to put spiritual formation at the heart of theological education without impairing any of its academic rigor. In designing its new curriculum, the Bexley faculty was aided by a retrieval of core assumptions in the Anglican tradition itself, convictions that fairly invite putting spiritual formation at the heart of theological education. For a fuller treatment of the assumptions underlying this perspective, I refer the reader to my article, "Reflections on Spirituality in Anglican Theological Education," *Anglican Theological Review* LXXXI, 3 (Summer 1999), 429–49.
11. Syllabus APT 623 Group Spiritual Direction, 1.
12. Rose Mary Dougherty, S.S.N.D., *Group Spiritual Direction: Community for Discernment* (New York: Paulist Press, 1995).
13. The Triduum refers to the three-day period that begins with Maundy Thursday, continues through Good Friday and Holy Saturday, and ends with the Easter Vigil.
14. Cf. *Procedures and Requirements.*
15. Course evaluations are anonymous, but some students do sign their names. Where I have used comments from a signed course evaluation, permission to quote has been obtained.
16. Smith, "Spiritual Formation," 89.
17. Van den Blink, "Reflections on Spirituality," 437–38.

Appendix:
Class Bibliography

Bondi, Roberta C. *To Pray and to Love: Conversations on Prayer with the Early Church.* Minneapolis, MN: Fortress Press, 1991, Chapter 3, "Approaching Prayer," 47–74.

Bonhoeffer, Dietrich. *Life Together* (New Edition). San Francisco: Harper & Row, 1996.

Dougherty, Rose Mary. *Group Spiritual Direction.* New York: Paulist Press, 1995, Introduction, Chapters 1 through 7 and Epilogue, 3–47.

Fischer, Kathleen. *Women at the Well: Feminist Perspectives on Spiritual Direction.* New York: Paulist Press, 1988, Browse around.

Gratton, Carolyn. *The Art of Spiritual Guidance.* New York: Crossroad, 1992, Introduction and Chapters 1 through 5, 1–91.

Guenther, Margaret. *Holy Listening: The Art of Spiritual Direction.* Boston: Cowley, 1992, Introduction and Chapters 1 through 4, 1–140.

Hall, Thelma. *Too Deep for Words: Rediscovering Lectio Divina.* New York: Paulist Press, 1988, Chapters 1 through 4, 7–56.

Leech, Kenneth. *Soul Friend* (New Edition). San Francisco: Harper & Row, 1992, Chapters 1 through 3, 5–136.

May, Gerald. *Care of Mind/Care of Soul.* San Francisco: Harper & Row, 1992, Chapters 2, 3, 4, 5, and 6, 18–122.

Smith, Martin L. *The Word Is Very Near You: A Guide to Praying with Scripture.* Cambridge, MA: Cowley, 1989, Suggest you read all Part I but browse around.

Group Spiritual Direction on Capitol Hill

Doug Tanner

I am a fifty-four-year-old United Methodist minister. I'm also a
Southerner; my mother is from Virginia, my father from North
Carolina, where I was born and reared. My early religious background was one of somewhat typical Southern evangelical piety.
I answered an altar call when I was ten, though I'll never know
whether I was moved more deeply by the strains of "Softly and
Tenderly, Jesus Is Calling" or by the fact that the visiting
preacher—who was also a baseball scout for a nearby Methodist
college—had several autographed baseballs, one by my hero
Stan Musial. I intended to become a naval officer until the
summer of 1963, between my junior and senior years in high
school. That July and August, in Methodist youth activities, I
was moved clearly and profoundly by the spiritual depth of the
civil rights movement. The experiences of that summer transformed my perspective radically and set me on the path of

becoming an ordained minister. Over the years, it has become clear to me that my calling has always been to be an instrument of transformation that is both personal and social and has political consequences.

That kind of a calling is deeply within the Methodist tradition, dating back to John Wesley. The way I've been led to follow my personal calling has made me something of a maverick in my own ecclesiastical institution; my bishops and other superiors have given me space to do it. I've been a campus minister and a parish minister, but for most of the past twenty years, my ministry has been among people professionally engaged in politics. It is in that context that I have received most of my experience in group spiritual direction.

My first experience of spiritual direction in a group, though, came before I knew to name it by that particular term. In my late twenties, I had entered the early stages of activist clergy burnout. I had allowed my life to become depleted of both soul and spirit by feverishly pursuing "world-saving" tasks I perceived as my duty. At a retreat led by the Wellspring mission group of Washington's Church of the Saviour, I began to learn to pray at a much deeper level. I began to understand the concept of my "inward journey" as the source of clarity and direction for my "outward journey." I came to trust that, with faithful companions, I could discern the particular tasks to which I was called and trust God to call other people to the other tasks that, important as they might be, were not mine. And I learned that in and following that discernment, I would be given energy, resources, and direction for each step of the way.

Doug Tanner

When I was thirty-five, I was asked to manage a congressional campaign for a friend who also was acquainted with much of the same wisdom through the same source. I certainly didn't know how to run a campaign for dog catcher, let alone Congress, but at that stage my friend Robin Britt, a fellow Democrat from Greensboro, North Carolina, didn't have enough money to hire anyone who did. I learned, several things broke our way, and Robin won by a comfortable margin in the fall of 1982. I came to Washington with him as a senior aide, with the internally understood assignment of helping him stay true to his deeper self as he navigated his way through all of the pressures and pitfalls of congressional life. That task proved harder than winning a campaign. In spite of our good and serious intentions, both of us slipped into letting our greatest energies go into the variety of tasks that conventional political wisdom dictated as critical for Robin to retain and secure his seat. We wrote and mailed our newsletters. We sought and generated press coverage. And we raised money—more than twice what we had the first time. No one twisted our arms, nor did we do any particular thing we later came to regret. It was what we didn't do that shaped our course. We didn't take enough time; we didn't create enough structure or space; we didn't regularly or often enough gather our companions. Without all of those, we could neither listen to the Spirit, hear its invitation, nor follow its direction.

I came out of the whole experience with a much greater appreciation of how hard it can be in the realm of day-to-day political life to make room for spiritual discernment. I also came out of it with a better sense of some ways in which that difficulty might be diminished—at least somewhat. Five years later, after a sojourn as a parish minister and director of a retreat center on the eastern shore of the Chesapeake Bay in Virginia, I had returned to Washington to explore the possibilities.

In the winter of 1988, I met a then-freshman congressman, Glenn Poshard, from southern Illinois. Although it was not what I knew to expect of someone from a fundamentalist Southern Baptist background, Glenn had read a lot of Thomas Merton and had made retreats at the Abbey of Gethsemani in Kentucky, where Merton lived and wrote. Experiencing some of the typical loneliness of a new member of Congress and hungry for spiritual companionship, Glenn readily responded to my suggestion that we gather a couple more companions and embark on a spiritual journey together. I recruited two other friends I knew to be spiritually sensitive and actively engaged in politics.

The four of us began to meet in Glenn's office at 7:30 on Wednesday mornings for an hour and a half of something close to what I later learned to call group spiritual direction. We began with a few minutes of silence, followed by a brief reading, and then sat together until someone was led to say something. Those first words almost invariably emerged from the depths of the speaker's soul. I then sought to facilitate the conversation in a way that would keep it at that deeper level. We shared insights and questions and soon came to trust each other with the struggles and the major decisions of our lives.

I came out of the experience confident that similar groups could be equally valuable to a number of Glenn's congressional colleagues and their staff members. I knew that the personal crises and decisions would be different. But everyone in political life (and every other realm of life) has points at which the challenge of being true to one's deepest self is daunting and almost insurmountable without the resources of regular time for discernment with sensitive and trustworthy companions. I also was confident that I possessed political knowledge, pastoral sensitivities, and gifts as a group facilitator that could equip me to bring together other similar groups on Capitol Hill. What I didn't know was where I would find the time. If I was going to do much more, it would come out of my "tent-making" work as Deputy Director of a national voter registration and education organization, and I would either need to be paid for it or find a way to subsidize it. (For those unfamiliar with the reference, Saint Paul supported himself by making tents as he traveled and preached.

In a leap of faith, the four of us involved in the original group founded a consciously interfaith, nonpartisan, and nonprofit organization called the Faith & Politics Institute in 1991. Our mission has been to offer occasions for moral reflection and spiritual community to people in political life, to value civility and respect as spiritual values essential to democracy, and to strengthen public leadership that seeks to heal the nation's divisive wounds (most notably those related to race). The organization now has a full-time staff of six and a thirty-member board of directors. We raise our own money from a wide range of individuals, foundations, religious organizations, corporations, and labor unions. While "reflection groups" and retreats for members of Congress and their staffs are only one part of our program, they are at the center.

At several points along the way over the past ten years, there have been amazingly graced moments in which I have known not only that this is what I've been meant to do but also that God has been very present with me in doing it. One of those came at the Shalem workshop on Group Spiritual Direction in which I participated. Several have come in memorable meetings of the Faith & Politics Institute reflection groups I facilitate. Last year, a retreat sponsored by the Thomas Merton Foundation at the Abbey of Gethsemani was the occasion of a sharp awareness of God's presence and guidance. At too many other points, I've allowed myself to ignore or forget those moments. I've carried the burdens of developing the organization as though they were all on my back. I've become as hurried, harried, and ungrounded as my friends whom I would help discover a different way to live. But the graced moments do come. Moreover, I think I may finally be learning that the more I open myself to them, the more often they arrive.

At this point, there are four groups for members of Congress and four groups for congressional staff. I meet with each of the member groups, often with a cofacilitator. Other facilitators meet with the congressional staff groups, and sometimes I also am present with one. Each group is composed of four to eight participants, and meets for an hour—usually early in the morning—in an office or small meeting room on Capitol Hill. Time is an especially precious commodity for our participants; the meeting starts promptly and ends on time. We begin with a few minutes of meditative music, conscious breathing, and a brief reading. After the reading, we sit in silence until someone is led to speak; sometimes it's a few seconds, sometimes a few minutes. After that, the chief challenge to the facilitators is to keep the conversation at the depth in which it begins. We do not carefully divide the time among the participants; there simply isn't enough of it in an hour to do so and have the portion be ample. Instead, we see that everyone is brought into the conversation roughly equally and make it clear that any major event, question, or decision that any participant is experiencing in a given week has precedence over the reading as a subject for the group. As closing time nears, the facilitator often checks to see if anyone has a particular concern about which he or she has not yet spoken but wishes to share with the group. We then stand, join hands, and share a closing prayer. Early in the life of a group, it is usually one of the facilitators who offers the closing prayer. As the group matures, it's usually one of the participants.

Not every participant is present every week; occasionally there is a competitive demand to which they need to defer. Most participants, though, are there most of the time. Given the scheduling demands on members of Congress and many congressional staff, the fact that participants return week after week is rather remarkable. Participants often call the meeting "the best hour of the week," and some speak of it as the only reflective time they have. However that may make you feel about the way your government is run (!), the sessions clearly speak to a genuine hunger in the souls of the participants.

I sometimes am asked how the groups got started. There isn't a uniform answer. Some came when I perceived a need and interest in a given member, and he or she and I considered others whom we had a hunch might be a good fit and be open to the experience. We then recruited and worked out the time and place as we went. Others resulted from my sending a letter with a response form throughout the House of Representatives. When a member returned the response form, I arranged a personal one-on-one meeting in which we discussed the nature of the group, possible times to meet, and other potential participants. I then put the group together with an eye toward mixing religious backgrounds, races, seniority levels, genders, and, insofar as possible, parties and ideologies. Having checked on available times and whether there was anyone with whom a given member definitely did not want to gather, I then followed my intuition concerning personalities that would clash or complement.

About four years ago, I recruited a variety of clergy friends in the Washington area to serve voluntarily as cofacilitators. The assembled team included two women (one Presbyterian and one Episcopalian) and five men (two Jesuits, one rabbi, one United Methodist, and the dean of a prominent predominantly African American Protestant seminary). I led a morning-long orientation session and took care of the logistical arrangements in placing cofacilitators with groups. All seven participated for at least a season, with some exhibiting greater gifts, talents, and knowledge for the work than others. Two have since moved out of town, and the life circumstances of two more changed to limit their availability. The other three are still engaged with the work. In the meantime, we have added two more clergy to the Faith & Politics staff. Both are good with groups and share the facilitation load. In the last Congress, other dimensions of our work at the

241

institute took precedence over expanding the group offerings. Now, however, that is about to change, and I am giving more attention to recruiting, orienting, and maintaining a team of facilitators. Along with the qualities required of any competent group director, ours need to be reasonably astute observers of national politics and to possess a measure of sense about the spiritual struggles particular to public officials—without being awed or overly impressed by anything about the Capitol Hill scene. Credentials from a recognized religious institution also help establish credibility in this particular arena. Add to that the requirement that they be willing to make their way to a Capitol Hill office at 7:30 or 8:00 in the morning, without a guaranteed place to park, and the field becomes limited. Still, there remain many prospective facilitators in Washington with all of these qualities. We simply need to connect with them, which is a matter of prayer, active searching, and discernment.

The challenges I face as one who seeks to be an instrument of group spiritual direction in the often crazy context of congressional life are multiple. Some are logistical. Scheduling anything is always subject to changes in the congressional schedule. My staff has to call each week to determine who will be present and whether there will be a sufficient number for the group to meet.

Through my work with this process, I have become aware that our deep political divisions can be bridged when people are willing to meet each other in a common desire. While this is not the primary purpose of our being together, I cannot help but appreciate this as a fruit of our being together. This raises other challenges, such as, Do we hold out to make each group bipartisan? When a bipartisan group really works, sorely needed bridges are built, and members are reminded of their common humanity in a setting where they're more often encouraged to demonize each other. (One morning a Democratic member confessed to a Republican colleague, "It's better when you're here. When you aren't, we act like Democrats!") On the other hand, establishing trust in any political context is inherently difficult, and doing so across party lines can be so hard that the group never comes together as well as it would on one side of the aisle or the other. I'm still working this one through. It's generally not as much of an issue at the staff level as it is for the members. The best solution may be to offer a variety of combinations, encouraging consciously bipartisan as far as possible.

Probably the greatest challenge of all, though, is continually remembering, trusting, and relearning that this work isn't simply a worthy project of a worthy organization. When I prepare well for each session…when I pray regularly for the participants…when I fully open myself to the Spirit, I see that the project and the organization are instruments of something much greater, much more powerful, much more lasting. Sometimes it is only my eyes from which the scales fall. At other times, they fall away from those of every participant in the room. We see each other face to face and know in our bones what Merton meant when he spoke of the "hidden wholeness" in all things. The opportunity to be with participants living through stages of their lives and sometimes making critical decisions in that awareness is rewarding beyond measure.

Doug Tanner

How do I live my life in a way that opens me to the Spirit, when the Faith & Politics Institute's organizational demands sometimes seem as heavy to me as those that bear on any member of Congress? I do this, I think, by both embracing a healthy spiritual discipline for myself and forgiving myself when I fail to keep it, just as I would encourage any of the congressional participants to do. If I am to teach others who carry heavy external demands, I can hardly expect my own life to be one in which time and space for contemplation is easily, readily, and abundantly available. Sometimes we have to grab spiritual community on the run. At the same time, I'm learning that just as a member of Congress has to set aside certain times for re-election tasks, I have to set aside certain times for deepening of my own consciousness and renewal of my own spirit. It's best when that leads to a combination of daily meditation, regular (for example, monthly) meetings with a spiritual guide (or group), and one or two annual retreats, each of which lasts several days. When I am reasonably faithful to that discipline, I see and sense evidence of the hidden wholeness that sustains and energizes me. When I am not, I often miss it. When I not only see and sense the hidden wholeness but also am able to help others from a wide range of religious traditions to glimpse and embrace it, then I know my place in the universe.

V.

=========

Core Understandings in Group Spiritual Direction

When Lynne Smith and I started leading workshops in group spiritual direction, we usually began by describing the process in its entirety. Then we would "unpack" each part of the process, sharing what led us to do it this way. Finally, we would give participants an experience of the process.

This never really worked very well. It seemed to hook people in a shared vulnerability: a need to "get it right." We would be halfway through describing the process and someone reading from a notebook would ask, "Could you just go back a second? Was that three minutes or four minutes of silence after a person has shared?" We would be in the midst of an actual time of group spiritual direction when a person would turn to a facilitator and

245

say, "Is this an appropriate question for me to ask?" Or, when commenting on the process after the experience of it, someone might say, "The silences weren't long enough. I didn't have time to think of what I wanted to say."

After several times of presenting the material this way, we realized that people were missing the heart of what we wanted to convey. We rearranged the parts of the workshop. Shortly after the beginning, we would invite people into an extended time of silence together, inviting them into a place of openness for whatever might be given them for their prayer for themselves during this time. We then moved people into the small groups they would be in for spiritual direction, where they could begin to share briefly and informally a little of their spiritual journeys. We suggested that they might want to share something that had come to them in the silence or something of what drew them to the workshop. We described spiritual community and posed the possibility that, for the few days of the workshop, the group might become a spiritual community. We encouraged them to cultivate an intercessory attitude, allowing spacious silence within their listening, so they could make space for God's prayer within them for each person they were hearing. We also included a different experience of intercessory prayer.

Only after this introduction did we talk directly about the process of group spiritual direction and guide people through it. And, as much as we could tell, people really seemed to "get" what it was about. We noticed a difference in the feedback on evaluation forms. When we asked people to tell us about one idea or question that they took with them from the workshop, responses to the original workshop format would usually center around details. We would hear things like, "I tend to lose track of time. I'll need to get a stop watch." "I liked the prayers you used. I want to find a book of prayers I can use to begin the silence in my group at home." People who participated in the workshop in its new form raised questions and insights like, "I keep wondering how I can live intercessory prayer at home the way I have lived it here," or "I'm beginning to pray about where I can find spiritual community at home," or "I know I need more silence in my life."

The learnings from those early days of group spiritual direction workshops have served me well. When I was writing the book, *Group Spiritual Direction: Community for Discernment*, some people said to me, "This book would probably be more popular if you would write it as a handbook, a 'how to' for group spiritual direction. At least you should include a 'question and answer' section which would tell people how to deal with problems in group spiritual direction as they arise." I couldn't do that. I felt it would betray the very heart of group spiritual direction.

Group spiritual direction is not about getting someone else's answers or mimicking a process even if it doesn't fit for us. Rather, it is about the cultivation of a discerning heart in all of life, an intercessory stance, if you will. It's about finding a community of friends who are willing to be present to God for one another in the silence and dialogue of active listening. It's about finding out together what fits for us as the unique persons we are in God. I wanted the book to serve as a vehicle of discernment for those considering group spiritual direction.

Rose Mary Dougherty

So, too, I would like this book to be a vehicle of discernment for those who are considering group spiritual direction. I want to underscore once again the heart of the process and its grounding in an understanding of spiritual community, intercessory prayer, and the silence of spacious listening. Most of the experiences of group spiritual direction described in this book flow from an appreciation of these concepts. It seemed well to address them directly, however, and the following essays do just that.

Rose Mary Dougherty

Experiencing Spiritual Community in Different Settings

Trudy Dervan

Dawn has not yet broken through the darkness as a handful of monks and two of us, visitors, gather for vigils in the tiny oratory in northeastern Pennsylvania. Our chanting of the psalms brings light to our hearts; together we ponder the readings of the day. In shared silence, we return to our individual spaces to await morning prayer and Mass. Our private prayers weave a thick blanket of reverent silence that lies over the house.

There is something that draws me every year to this tiny community in the Poconos. The shared psalms, the comfortable and expansive silence that stretches between, the bread broken together at Mass and at meals: the ordinariness of daily life as expressed in monastic community is rather like an illuminated manuscript—it's really just another text but so very different in its vibrancy.

As I look back over my life, I can clearly see this call to—and deep need for—spiritual community. My spiritual quest began, in fact, with the drive to satisfy the need for community.

At the age of thirty-eight, I found myself living apart from my husband of fifteen years. On weekdays, our children stayed with him in the house we had shared. My previously well-ordered life had become what felt like a blasted wasteland. A private person, I had never shared my marital troubles with anyone. Friends and family were stunned into a frightened distance. I had no one to turn to.

In the midst of this barren place, an acquaintance invited me to Christmas Eve Mass at a local Catholic church. My assumptions as a lifelong Protestant were blown away that night as I saw the living body of Christ praying and warmly reaching out to one another. And, most astounding, I discovered a searing hunger for the Eucharist that has never left me. A year later, I had become Catholic and joined that same parish.

It was in this parish family that I learned about real community. There is an open acceptance in this spiritual community of who I am, what the nature of my journey is, and how I may see God operating in my life. All things are imbued with the effects of this love, which creates trust, good will, and respect. I am quite certain that it is this firm grounding in community that has led me to the three major sources of nourishment for my spirituality today—the Cursillo Movement, companioning others on their spiritual journeys, and seeking out the monastic community for my annual retreat.

The vibrancy of spiritual community is expressed in love that, for me, is centered in shared beliefs and traditions. At the same time, there is a sense of mutual accountability coupled with acceptance of what is real and true for each of us. Finally, spiritual community always expects the best of me, and it listens with me to discern what is the best for me. To the extent that this happens, a spiritual community also becomes spiritual director. It was in my parish community and in my Cursillo small sharing group—called Group Reunion—where I first encountered what I now know to be spiritual direction in a group setting. Of course, neither of those communities represents the experience of a formal spiritual direction relationship. But it has become obvious in hindsight, with the knowledge that I have gained in my own training as a spiritual guide, that these communities offered a form of spiritual direction.

It was in this parish community that I discerned my call to become Catholic. There was never any pressure applied, no pros-elytizing—simply a sitting with me through the process of my own discernment. This community also supported me through the process of annulling my first marriage, a difficult but worthwhile process. But, more important than the annulment, I had something new: a rock-solid faith and commitment to my church that even disappointment and the prospect of a lonely future could not shake. My community celebrated with me—not for the annulment but for my newfound strength in and reliance on God.

Spiritual direction and spiritual community are interdependent. Ever-deepening bonds between friends and with God can lead a reflective and prayerful community to a methodology of group spiritual direction. "When individuals take seriously the responsibility to stay grounded in the Mystery of Love, a group can give itself to the process of group spiritual direction."[1] Margaret Guenther says that spiritual direction is about "'holy listening,' presence and attentiveness."[2] I continue to experience these qualities, so fundamental to the spiritual direction process, in my committed, loving and prayerful communities.

Rose Mary Dougherty defines the elements of spiritual direction as (1) God inviting people to be together; (2) God gifting each person through the presence of the other; (3) the directee assuming responsibility for his or her own life with God; and (4) members supporting each other in prayer.[3]

Several years after my first marriage was annulled, I met my husband-to-be when he joined our parish family. Once again my community was with me as I went through yet another discernment: Did I really want to remarry? Through the long process of my coming to embrace my call to be a married person again, my parish community sat with me, listened to God and me, prayed for us as a couple and as individuals, and waited. The joy they shared with us on our wedding day was a culmination of the discernment we shared.

Over this time, spanning nearly ten years from the day I attended my first Mass to the day I was married again, I learned that a commitment to prayer, an open heart, patience with process, and respect and acceptance for others in a spiritual setting allowed me, also, to offer guidance. I supported numerous others in their faith struggles, their discernments, their joys and sorrows while at the same time I sensed God gifting me through them. This "blessing of reciprocity present in the bond of spiritual community"[4] happens in God. It is also found in my Cursillo Group Reunion.

The Cursillo Movement's aim is evangelization, and its appeal lies in its tightly knit and dynamic Christian community. The foundation of the Cursillo Movement and the key to its effectiveness is the support provided to Cursillistas by small faith sharing and accountability groups called Group Reunions, also known as Friendship Groups. The centrality of these groups to the Cursillo method of life cannot be overstated. In the Cursillo Group Reunion, "the friends must be deeply motivated to pursue their growth in both their spiritual development and relationships with each other."[5]

My own Group Reunion has had the same core participants, enhanced by the comings and goings of several others, for more than a dozen years. It has always had a strong affinity for silent prayer, committed listening, and prayerful feedback. For some reason, we have never been drawn to problem solving, group therapy, work-related discussions, gossip, or the other dead ends that small groups can easily slide into. Over time, we individually encountered the practice of contemplative prayer that led us to collective silence and reflective listening.

My own prayer evolved into contemplation through a clear call to silence, to sitting, to waiting. Years of silent retreats spent in contemplative community have strengthened my commitment to this form of prayer and affirmed my call to it. Another of our group was gifted with an experience of contemplative prayer quite spontaneously while on a chapel visit during a Cursillo Weekend. His experience revealed a whole new way of being with God; it has changed his prayer life forever. Yet another has come to the contemplative experience more gradually. She is equally happy with spoken communal prayer as with long silences.

Over the years, we have been witnesses to each other's evolving prayer lives and relationships with God. The evolution into a group contemplative experience was a small next step. It seemed natural; it seemed to be God's will for us.

Our contemplative Group Reunion is marked by extended prayer, both silent and spoken, at the outset. Each participant speaks fully, covering the whole week, while the others listen "as Christ." Prayerful silence ensues, as each participant opens his or her heart and mind to what God might have to offer the speaker in response to what was shared. Sometimes there is nothing that surfaces; other times a response of wisdom and clarity is forthcoming; always the mood is one of gracious attendance to each other. At the end, silent and spoken prayer and prayers of petition are offered. The time, while constrained to about an hour, feels expansive. There is no rush; we operate in God's time. Our trust in each other, in God's presence, and the sanctity of our shared space are implicit.

As in any spiritual community, the quality that separates a "regular" Group Reunion from one that may be engaged in group spiritual direction is the absence of self in the listening and responding. In contemplative community, the emphasis is on listening to God, hearing Christ in each other's words, being present in a loving and nonjudgmental way to the reality of the other. It is this setting aside of one's preoccupations and preconceptions, with the deliberate attempt to be a clear channel for God's listening, God's loving, and God's response, that sets contemplative community apart from the norm.

It is the prayerfulness of the members and their attention to their own formation that keeps our Group Reunion on course. Without individual spiritual direction and regular retreats, the group might need a leader, as in other models, or fall into problem solving, group therapy, or, worst of all, bad advice given as though it were God's. As it is, all the members serve as facilitators concurrently; everyone remembers to check the clock from time to time, and everyone is accountable for keeping the group on course. Faithfulness in attendance and trust in confidentiality are of utmost importance.

These same qualities are what pull me back to the small monastic community each year. Living in monastic life shows me once again the way that intentional spiritual community can evolve to reflect some qualities of spiritual direction. We honor each other's purpose in being in this place at this particular time; there is no invasion of privacy; there are no pre-set expectations for performance here; careful listening is required.

Living this way allows the monks always to be prayerfully present to God, and of course, that is what differentiates truly spiritual community from all other types of community. Beyond a constant openness to what God may be saying regarding any situation, significant or mundane, there is an expansiveness of time. The simplicity of life allows for this expansive sense inside the ordered and rhythmic framework of the Divine Office.

Trudy Dervan

In our spiritual friendships also there is no rushing. We are sensitive to all things operating in "God's time," not our own. True spiritual community is strengthened when God's time is honored, and we are present to one another for as long as it takes. The cast may change from one gathering to the next, but the expansiveness of time is always honored. We listen carefully, aware of God's presence and with one ear tuned to God's "channel." Undergirding all this is the shared love of God and friend.

In darkness again at the end of the day, my friend and I lift our soft voices with the monks' as we sing the Compline Hymn of Night Prayer. We are a small band, huddled together against the dark in the reflected light of the tabernacle candle. But there is strength and real clarity here—strength that comes from shared faith and the honoring of each person, clarity that is the result of careful listening to each other and to God. Most of this group is here for the long term, committed to the ongoing process of growing in love of God and their sisters and brothers.

My friend and I share that commitment in our busy secular lives. It won't be such a big step, returning to "ordinary" life. For while monastic community may seem archaic or radical to some, it really is a lens through which I can view my own communities and clearly see the gifting that takes place in them. In both places, I am standing on holy ground.

Notes

1. Rose Mary Dougherty, *Group Spiritual Direction* (New York: Paulist Press, 1995), 55.

2. Margaret Guenther, *Holy Listening* (Boston: Cowley, 1992), 1.
3. Dougherty, *Group Spiritual Direction*, 18–19.
4. Ibid., 13.
5. National Secretariat of the Cursillo Movement in the United States, *Leaders' Manual*, 173.

Intercessory Prayer and Group Spiritual Direction

Don MacDougall

In spiritual direction, it is one thing to be open to where a person may generally be with God, to watch and listen with God for the movements of someone toward or away from God, and perhaps even the movements of God in the person. It is another thing to become more open to what God may wish for the person and to join with God in that desire and follow where it leads. The first has to do with the art of discernment, the latter with "intercessory prayer." This essay will focus on the latter, although what we will probably discover, as we set out to pray for someone, is that the quality of our discernment in spiritual direction will change as well.

In my experience, the biggest challenge in intercessory prayer is the willingness to practice it, to simply do it. As we shall see, it involves our whole selves, truly, and our own willingness to enter in to being with God for another. It means letting go more of the smaller, self-centered self in the process. If you are anything like I am, you will resist the cost of that at some point.

Close behind simply doing it is the challenge of understanding what it is we think we are doing when we pray for someone else. Or for that matter, what do we actually believe about the way God really is with the world and us, and with those we pray for, and how intercessory prayer can be a part of that? Are we truly "interceding" with God, as the word suggests—trying to change God's mind perhaps; asking God to do something different from what God would otherwise do if we didn't ask? Further, if what we think we are looking for is God's will in the matter, is God playing "now you see it, now you don't" with us about what God's will is, and we have to ask just right for God to finally pull it out from behind God's back? If personal resistance to the cost of praying for others doesn't stop us, then questions such as these might be close behind. In fact, I think they lurk in the minds of many people. Having a reasonably integrated view of the way God is with the world is important if intercessory prayer is going to feel like an authentic undertaking. Without such a view, sooner or later we will find ourselves pretending or faking intercessory prayer, and we probably will stop doing it.

Let's start, however, with the *practice* of intercessory prayer if for no other reason than not to be caught in the Western habit of trying to figure it out first, then mistaking our understanding for the reality and perhaps never getting around to actually doing it. More of the reality of intercessory prayer will be found in the practice of it and not in the thinking about it. As we set out to practice it more intentionally, its mysteries, challenges, satisfactions, and costs will reveal themselves soon enough.

The first thing I notice about intercessory prayer (after the first flush of enthusiasm and especially when praying for someone at a distance or for someone I don't know very well) is that I simply don't want to do it. That is, I don't want to go very far into it. It takes effort. It takes concentration. It takes time.

If all it means is rattling off a bunch of names on a list, then that might be all right. But if it means something more, if it means getting into who they really are, and what they are really struggling with, and what their relationship really might be with God, then that quickly begins to feel like work.

Initially this resistance seems simply to come from personal difficulties such as making the effort or worrying about becoming emotionally involved with others. But after a while I realize I also have to let go of what I start out wanting for others, or what they may seem to want for themselves, and have to begin to ask God how God sees the situation and what God might wish for them.

On the one hand, this makes it easier and is a relief, since the realization grows that I'm not responsible for "making it all right" with my praying. God is the one to do that. But what if it starts to appear that God doesn't "want" to do that either, or simply isn't going to, for whatever reason—what then? Even the expectation of it being made "all right" through prayer becomes part of the problem. Suddenly it is difficult again, since I am now entering into a fuller realization of the situation and finding myself called to share and bear, along with God, the uncertainty and confusion, the joy and celebration, perhaps even the pain and suffering that may be there.

At that point, in addition to whatever else I am feeling, I can start to feel anxious, but anxious not necessarily for the people for whom I am praying. They may be fine, or at least relatively unaware. The anxiety comes from having to let go of my little, self-sufficient self, to stand more side by side with God, and from having to see and bear the human condition as expressed in the lives of these people—to hear it and bear it as God hears it and bears it, as much as I can. This is a cost I wasn't expecting. It means having to let myself go more to God, which wasn't part of the deal in my understanding when I set out comfortably to pray for these people in the first place! Why does it always have to end up with me and where I am with God? But that is what it means. So intercessory prayer becomes a challenge, an invitation to enter more fully into God, myself, in the process. It means moving further out of the comfortable, secure place I have built for myself. In fact, I can't go very far into intercessory prayer, authentically, without allowing this to happen. No wonder there is anxiety! No wonder there is resistance!

All of this is in reference to praying for someone who is at a physical or emotional distance. What about when they are sitting with me in a group and the purpose of being together is spiritual direction? That starts out again being easier, since the stimulation of the group context takes care of the willingness to take the time, make the effort, become emotionally interested in them. They are sitting right there with me. The larger and deeper challenges, however, come more quickly to the fore: letting myself go more to God as the enriching source of any intervention I might make, rather than simply jumping in with the first comment that occurs to me; letting go of what I may initially want for them or what they may superficially want for themselves; asking God how God sees the situation, what God may have in mind, and being open to going with what may come. This again gets me into the quality of my own immediate givenness, my own presence and responsiveness to God, my willingness to be there as a companion with God, with its implicit cost of bearing, of holding the person. It makes spiritual direction a deeply prayerful act and not merely a technical achievement, an act that invites my whole self in relation with God.

It is out of that quality of immediate givenness of myself to God that urgings and nudges, hints, phrases, images, and questions may come. With discernment and quiet, what unfolds may prove fruitful—the more so when it happens in a group in which each one is seeking to be immediately given to God for the others.

So, practicing intercessory prayer involves noticing and facing the anxiety, the resistance involved in giving over more of myself to God. It means noticing the anxiety, letting it be, and, as much as my heart will allow, being present with God and staying open to whatever God may be trying to do in the person.

However, in addition to difficulties with practice, there also may be intellectual uncertainties, questions, and distortions (of which we may hardly be aware) that also can act as "spoilers" to our getting on with it. As I said earlier, it is important to "have a view," a reasonably integrated sense of the way God may actually be with the world and with us and our affairs, and what prayer may have to do with that. But what if we no longer believe some of the pieces of the worldview that is lodged in our brains?

One possibility of such difficulty is buried in the word *intercessory* itself. Do you share this problem with me? It sounds to me as if the word comes from the feudal or monarchical days when people who had some political influence with those in power "interceded" on behalf of those who didn't. The effort would be to secure favor from the strong for the weak, to get the wealthy to share with the poor, to change the attitude of the powerful to the powerless, and it was considered the natural way of things for it to be that way.

Is that what intercessory prayer is about? Are we interceding with a powerful and distant God, to change God's mind to be more merciful and caring toward the one for whom we are praying? Is the act of intercessory prayer, then, an act of getting the words right, of having the proper posture of submission and supplication, or even of getting our heart, our emotions wound up to the right degree of intensity, so that God will hear and respond as we would like? I doubt that! What then?

A closely related question concerns how we may see "the will of God." Is intercessory prayer an exercise in finding out what "the will of God" is, as if it is established and unchanging, and then conforming to it, or urging acceptance of it on someone else? Well-educated and otherwise thoughtful people will often talk about God's will that way, for themselves and others, especially at funerals and other experienced intrusions of mortality. If this is true, then God's mind is made up about a lot of things and has been since the beginning of creation. And if that's the case, what is the point of the whole thing? Is life one great big game of hide-and-seek, with us always seeking God's established will and never anything new under the sun?

I doubt that too! What then?

I think these two closely related concerns, and the belief system about God, creation, human life, and prayer implicit in them, are part of people whether we are overtly religious or not. But these concerns can profoundly spoil our view of what we think we are doing when we set out to pray for someone else. They will sap the energy and dynamism, the belief and commitment, that might otherwise be in such praying.

Over the centuries, there have been many people who have moved further into life in God and who know directly that God is not distant and opinionated. Through their own experience, they have come to realize the opportunity in every moment, through prayer, for partnership, friendship, mutuality, family-member intimacy with God beyond our wildest dreams and our initial willingness to let go and enter in. They know about the creative possibilities for life that flow from there.

Yet there is an antiquated belief system still afoot in the world that sees God as distant, perceives God's will as rigidly established, believes human life is a frantic search for that absolute will, and that prayer when done right is a magical way of finding and conforming to that will. Since most of us sense we can't do it "right," we feel confused and are tempted to give it up altogether.

Maybe it will be only through the reported experience of those great spiritual adventurers who go before the rest of us that we will come to know differently. Maybe it will be only through the flow and ebb, the surge and retreat of the spring and neap tides of the human spirit moving ever more fully into and out of God in the lived experience of humanity that we will come to know about how immediate, friendly, and open to us God is. Maybe it will be only through our own experience as we move through awakening, recognition, purification, surrender, and transformation that we will come to know we are brothers and sisters of God in creation.

We can add to this the growing human awareness of the nature of creation itself as open and dynamic, of the possibilities there are in the realization that we are invited to participate with God in its further unfolding, and of the dramatic significance of prayer in that realization.

"Behold I am doing a new thing. Even now it emerges. Do you not perceive it?" (Isa 43:19). If God is truly doing a new thing, then:

- What if, in the interest of fresh practice and fresh interpretation, we were to undertake praying for each other with the realization that God "waits" for just that act from us to open together a fresh petal in the rose of creation?

- What if the quality of the further flowering and fruiting of the whole world in God's image from this moment on relies upon our joining our desires and our energies with God's?

- What if "the will of God" is more "the desire of God" and the whole of creation arises out of God's love of being and making stuff and out of the desire of God for the companionship of beings who will love God out of their own freedom and be partners henceforth in the loving and creating?

- What if God doesn't know, and doesn't want to know yet, what the form and content of the next moment will be? What if God wants our company in creating together something new in the next moment, and in the interest of such creativity, "waits" for us to join in? Wouldn't that be a lot more engaging, for God and for us, if indeed it were that way?

If ongoing creation is indeed like that—dynamic, unfolding, open, and "waiting" for our fuller participation with God in its flowering—then the will or desire of God is more something to be joined than an objective, established reality to be found. If any of this is the way it is, the implications for prayer, and for praying for each other in particular, are tremendous. "Prayer" then is the willing, creative act of giving ourselves over, moment by moment—gifts, resistance, and all—to the larger possibility of creation that God and we together might bring about. That would be far more creative than banging about trying to find "the will of God," as if God's mind were made up one way forever. (What if we also dropped the phrase "intercessory prayer" and simply spoke of "praying for others"?)

My sense of God and creation informs and enables my prayer for others, and this is especially true in group spiritual direction. In group direction, what seems to draw me into this prayer and what keeps me there is the desire to be present and involved (along with God and others) in the flow of creation that goes on. It is a deep privilege and gift to be there, to attend it together, to be part of it with open awareness and compassion, and to contribute to it, with discernment, whatever seems to help the growing.

Sitting in a spiritual direction group with three or four others hardly feels dramatic. In fact, it seems rather ordinary. We sit in silence together. Someone speaks. We sit in silence with it. We respond. We sit in silence together. Someone else speaks. On it goes. Is this what creation is about? Probably it is, in the sense that we are praying for each other there and seeking to join with God in God's effort to bring these people we are accompanying into further being. What else could it be about?

Silence:
Opening Space for God

Margaret Benefiel and Susan Skillen

Jane enjoys retreats and quiet days. For several years, she has felt drawn more and more into solitude and silence. As her relationship with God has deepened, she has found herself yearning to share her experience with others in her church, but she doesn't know how. She attends a workshop on group spiritual direction and senses God inviting her to offer group spiritual direction in her church. She announces the group in the church bulletin, talks with interested people, and then meets with the five people who arrive for the first meeting. Although she had explained to everyone ahead of time the ground rules of group spiritual direction and the atmosphere of prayerful silence that would permeate the group, she discovers that silence is new to most members. She finds that, try as she might, she can't seem to move the group into the depth of silence she had hoped for. Although the members leave the first meeting telling Jane what a great meeting it was, Jane carries a vague sense of disappointment.

In her own prayer afterward, Jane realizes how much she wants group members to experience what she has. At the same time, she is reminded in her prayer that it has taken time for her to get to the level of comfort with silence that she has and that silence was very difficult for her at the beginning. As she brings each member of the group into her prayer, she feels compassion for each one and realizes that the process of moving more deeply into silence as a group will take time and patience and will be bumpy at times, just as her own process has been.

Readiness for prayerful silence begins with a longing for God. Jane herself gradually entered the world of solitude and silence because of her deep desire for God. Each of us carries within a deep desire and longing. Although we may not consciously identify either the source or the object of our longing, we all have a sense of desire, of wanting something more to satisfy our hearts. While we may attempt to soothe the urgency of desire with distraction or materialistic pursuits, when we quiet ourselves the desire rises to the surface. Desire is a passion that urges us to seek completeness and goodness. We long to be known and to be accepted as we are. Ultimately we long to be known by God, to know that we exist in God, and so our desire moves us toward God. At the same time fear may hold us back— fear of disappointment, rejection, betrayal, even annihilation. Cautiously we move toward God, prompted by desire, drawn by the "cords of love," yet resisting, hesitating, testing, all the way. Jane knew this dynamic within herself. She had learned to empty herself of the clutter within and allow her desire for God to surface. She knew the fears that rose up in her and that she could bring them into God's presence and allow God's love to dissolve them.

The members of Jane's group came because they, as Jane, experienced a longing for God. Jane's description of the group drew them. They desired intimacy with God and the opportunity to share with others who also sought that intimacy. Jane's life drew them, as well. They knew that they wanted what they saw in her. At the same time, they were afraid. This was new. They weren't sure about the silence part that Jane had described.

Twenty-first-century Western culture eschews silence. We Westerners grow up learning that our noisy, busy lives give us significance in the world. Asking us to let go of the noise and busyness and enter into silence is like asking us to give up our identities. As with the members of Jane's group, many who enter contemplative groups—whether they are spiritual direction groups, contemplative prayer groups, or discernment groups—have never before experienced group silence. Giving group members a taste of deep, prayerful silence is one of the greatest gifts a group leader can offer. It is also one of the greatest challenges a group leader faces.

The Gift of Prayerful Silence

In American culture, being comfortable with silence is usually something that we have to work to develop rather than something that comes naturally to us. Not only can it be uncomfortable, it may have undertones of anger from having experienced silence as either a seething angry presence or a silent abandonment. Silence may be something we try to avoid, by playing the radio or keeping the TV on for background noise. There is hardly any place we can go in our overly busy culture where silence is welcomed. Even out in the wilderness we can see hikers wearing Walkmans. Noise fills the void that we may feel about our own lives. It may distract us from facing the empty places within ourselves. In the din of our fast-paced existence, we can lose touch with our deeper selves, with who we truly are in God. In coming to group spiritual direction, the participants are seeking to connect to a deeper place within, connect to God, but for beginners in a contemplative approach to spiritual deepening, silence may feel very unsettling. Helping group members become comfortable with silence begins by giving them the gift of a new understanding and a new experience of silence.

For the person seeking to go deeper with God, silence can become a fullness rather than an emptiness. The image comes to mind of Elijah, who doesn't find God in the lightning, thunder or wind of the storm, but finally, in the stillness, hears the quiet voice of God. Turning down the distractions, without and within, that prevent the "still small voice" from being heard can help us learn to hear and recognize God's voice within. Changing our perception of silence as emptiness to experiencing it as being full of God's presence helps us begin to move into the silence as a welcoming and comforting space. This change may be difficult for some, but the repeated experience of finding silence to be safe and loving will be the best teacher.

Making silent space within for God's presence may mean taking time to do some housekeeping work of cleaning out the "clutter." As most of us discover, it can be very difficult to enter into prayerful silence with all the distractions and loose ends of our day competing for our attention. We may sometimes find ourselves in a battleground rather than peacefully resting in God's presence. Taking time at the beginning of one's prayer time to consciously "let go" of each item of clutter and give it to God can help clear the inner space for silence.

Clearing our inner space makes room for the activity of God's Spirit within us. Saint Teresa of Avila described our souls as gardens in which God pulls up weeds and plants the flowers. The prayer of quiet silence before God is the water that our flowers need in order to grow and bloom. In the hectic pace of our lives and the cacophony of so many words, these flowers become trampled, parched, and dry. Silence opens space for them to grow and gives water to nourish and refresh. Silence also helps us see ourselves as God sees us. We experience the loving gaze of God that reminds us that we are children of God, created in the divine image, in which the living force of our own creative energies are birthed in a natural inner rhythm that is true to who we are in God. Silence helps us attend to that true creative self—the gift of who we are created to be. Attentive inward listening in the open space of silence allows us to hear and respond to the gentle movements of God's Spirit drawing us, inviting us into a greater fullness and freedom of life.

Shared Silence and Listening

The role of silence in helping us listen to God and ourselves more clearly and fully is also important when we pray with others. In that prayerful silent space, it becomes possible to listen inwardly and outwardly at the same time. In shared silence, we learn to listen attentively to God for another person. We listen to the person speaking and listen to the inner movement of God's Spirit guiding and directing our thoughts and responses. In prayerful silence, we hold the other up to God and desire to hear as God hears, to see the other with God's eyes. We make space for God's Spirit to speak to us, listening for the ways in which God may be inviting the other into greater fullness and freedom.

Through listening deeply, we can help develop an inner silence, an inner space, which is able to receive the other. In effect, we can yield ourselves to the reality of the other so that one's reality is no longer "I" but "we." As we grow in listening attentively to the other, we can begin to hear, care, seek to understand, and desire to know in order to love. Open, attentive listening leads us to growth in which we can begin to accept the other unconditionally and let go of judging attitudes. We begin to discover that it is love itself that changes and transforms us, rather than judgment.

The development of one's own personal practice of silence is important in being able to bring that same attentive presence into shared silence and listening with another. In personal silent prayer, we may begin to experience that God listens to us, knows us, and loves us. This may be an uncomfortable experience, as we discover that God is inviting us into a deeper intimacy. We may find ourselves resisting or avoiding resting in silence in God's presence. There often is fear of exposure or vulnerability that rises to the surface when we are invited into intimacy. Honestly giving our fears to God and seeking to remain open to God's love can help us move toward that deeper relationship.

As we gradually learn to yield to God in response to God's love, we are able to receive more and more deeply the love that changes us into the wholeness of who God knows us to be. In the same way, our own open, attentive presence for the other is a kind of yielding of our own separateness and autonomy in order to be vessels of holy presence for the other. Through surrendered presence, we may become mirrors by which others see reflected their own selves as they are known by God; we may become voices speaking God's invitation into fullness and freedom; and we honor the uniqueness and dignity of the other.

Group Silence and Distractions

Listening to others with inner silence creates a space in which people can experience the safety and comfort necessary to grow toward intimacy with God and with one another. Such a spacious, loving silence provides the foundation for clearness committees (several people gathered in God's presence to help in personal discernment), corporate spiritual discernment (several gathered in God's presence seeking guidance about a matter of mutual concern), and group spiritual direction alike, and allows members to bring to group discernment the deeper areas of their lives.

Silence: Opening Space for God

Of course, it is highly likely that any group, no matter how spiritually mature or aware the members, will at times slip away from that quiet centeredness. The facilitator or any group member should not hesitate to gently call the group back into centeredness simply by requesting a few moments of silence. With practice and gentle prompting, the group can grow in its ability to maintain an atmosphere of prayerfulness in which all members seek to keep open that inner silent space within themselves.

Just as individuals may struggle with distractions in their own contemplative practice, spiritual direction groups will likely have times of struggling with distractions as well. Having realistic expectations for a beginning spiritual direction group means understanding that the group will need time to grow into silence and attentive listening through gentle teaching and guidance.

Learning silence also means developing a new way of being present. Often we think of presence as being present to someone. This usually involves conversation with the person. Through our presence, we want to communicate our love and acceptance of the other just as he or she is in that moment. We hope our presence is supportive of the being of the other, upholding the other. We are not often present to another in silence, because intentional silence for us usually means entering into one's own inner space rather than connecting with others in silence.

In the silence of which we have been speaking, however, we are inviting people to enter God's space, God's caring love. We are inviting them to be present to God with one another. In silence, we are attentive to God, entrusting one another to that caring love. Here we can let go of concerns about getting our communication right or even making another feel accepted and loved. We can want it for others, and it may well happen as people are able to let down some of their defenses in the silence, but this is not our primary reason for being together. Our reason for being together is our simple presence to God for one another, for whatever God might have in mind through us for one another. We are light for each other to see ourselves as we truly are in God. In silent presence, we allow God's loving presence to be the space in which we both are together, attentive to God and attentive to the other.

In group spiritual direction, discernment takes place in this atmosphere of silence and presence. When this atmosphere is there, the person presenting him- or herself for discernment is able to rest in the supportive, prayerful presence of the others. Resistance to allowing deeper thoughts and motivations into the light may be diminished. In this prayerful atmosphere, the anxious efforts on the group's part to "get it right" are lessened, and greater trust in the guidance of God's Spirit through the discernment process can develop. At times there will be disruptions in this atmosphere of silent presence, as when the group becomes sidetracked into problem solving or tangential topics. The facilitator's gentle request for a few minutes of silence can help reestablish the prayerful atmosphere. The facilitator does not need to make explanations to the group at this time, because that could quickly become a further distraction. Explanations and responses are better left for the evaluation time at the end when the group can take time to notice together how the flow of the discernment time went.

A Protected Space for Silence

What are some practical ways a leader can guide a group into silence? A leader provides guidelines for the group. Guidelines create a protected space, a space of safety. Like the wall of a garden that provides a protected space so the seeds can grow and the flowers can thrive, guidelines provide the safe space in which God's seeds can be planted and can grow in our hearts. A leader gives the guidelines and holds the protected space for the group. When the group members know the space is safe, they can relax and trust. They can move into silence. They can open to God. They know that the leader holds the space, so they don't have to be vigilant all the time. Feeling safe lets them dare to quiet their racing minds and hearts, dare to risk intimacy with God and with one another, dare to trust, to be honest, to care. Like the safety of the walled garden, the safety of the protected group space includes predictability, enough to know there won't be hostile intrusions. At the same time, the safety of the protected group space allows for the unpredictability of God's tenderly loving, surprise gifts.

The leader might open the first meeting with the simple exercise of inviting members into silence and into God's presence, naming some basic guidelines for the group, and then asking members to share what drew them to the group. Members can practice entering into the silence and using the basic guidelines as they listen to what drew each one to the group. Guidelines—such as, Listen through to the end of the sharing, allow a few moments of silence between speakers (the leader can

277

time this if necessary), listen with compassion, hold the person in God's presence in the silence after he speaks—can help a group move into silence and into God's presence. As the leader listens and gets a sense of how the members naturally adopt the guidelines and move into the silence, she can gauge the next step according to the group's need. The leader might pray to see the members as God sees them, attending to them tenderly. When fears arise in the group, God's compassion becomes the leader's compassion. Rather than feeling annoyed when group members have trouble moving into silence, he can learn to see the blocks and fears as a normal and hopeful part of the process. Members feel safe enough to voice fears and resistance, and often, in a safe space, can find healing. Gradually, then, they can move to deeper levels of silence, and the leader learns to know when and how to introduce longer periods of silence. The leader's tender compassion for the group helps invite them into the next step.

Conclusion

The experience of prayerful silence is an important part of a deepening life with God. As God lovingly draws us into that holy space, we begin to taste the gift of silence and to discover the peace for which we have been longing. Intentionally setting aside regular time and space in our lives for silence is a way of living that contrasts sharply with cultural norms. When we choose to ground the events and decisions of our lives in a silence that listens for what God is saying to us, we begin to move away from the cultural belief that we are autonomous, self-determining beings and toward a life that seeks intimacy and fulfillment in God. Having already tasted the goodness of experiencing God in silence, we want to share that goodness with others, inviting them into that deepening experience as well. Group spiritual direction is a way of inviting others into the experience of silence in a loving community that listens, encourages, cares and prays for one another. In the group, we create a place where growing into freedom can be protected and nourished, even though we may run into obstacles to building prayerful silence, just as we do in our individual lives. We can remember, however, that silence is a gift we receive from God; it is not something we do for ourselves. We can trust that, just as God is working in us through the gift of silence, God also will do the work in those to whom we offer God's invitation to silence.

Conclusion: "It Would Have Been Enough"

Rose Mary Dougherty, S.S.N.D.

As I come to the end of this book, having just reread all the essays, I am filled with awe and gratitude. The refrain of one of the prayers from the Passover Haggadah keeps echoing in my heart: "It would have been enough." If Yahweh had only called me to offer group spiritual direction, "it would have been enough." If group spiritual direction had never moved beyond the monthly meetings at Shalem, "it would have been enough." If the people who have come to our workshop in group spiritual direction were only to take it into their worshiping communities, "it would have been enough." But so much more has happened. So many people are recognizing the gifts of group spiritual direction and being called to offer it. They are using their creativity in adapting it to many segments of life. Its ripple effects are being felt far beyond its small beginnings at Shalem. It is enough.

Two weeks ago, I was preparing to lead a workshop in group spiritual direction for spiritual directors. I had been looking forward to my time with them. I knew some of the people who would be there and sensed it would be a time of mutual gifting. The day before I was to leave, I had to cancel because of illness. It was a difficult decision to make, but I had no choice. As I thought again of some of the people I knew who would be there, I kept saying to myself, "They can do this for one another. I hope they know it. At least some of them understand spiritual direction as I do. They know what spiritual community is about, and they've had experience of intercessory prayer. They have been in colleague groups that use Shalem's model, so they know what it's like to be present to God for one another in silence and in dialogue. They know the heart of it. They just need the experience, and the outline of the process can help with that. They can do it. I know they can." And they did.

The note I had from my contact with the group said, "God's presence and action was an awesome thing to witness these past days. I have come to a new understanding of intercessory prayer. I want to know it even more deeply and live the experience of it." These people responded to a call to come together. They were willing to share their prayer and their knowings and their wonderings. They were willing to wait together as the time unfolded. The Spirit was unleashed in their gathering. It was enough!

As I write this, I am aware that in many of our Christian churches we are preparing to celebrate the feast of Pentecost, the claiming by the early church of the Spirit's presence with us. The refrain we pray in our Eucharist this week is, "Lord, send out your Spirit and renew the face of the earth." A description of how people remembered the experience of the first Pentecost appears in the Acts of the Apostles:

> While the day of Pentecost was running its course, they were all together in one place,…and there appeared to them tongues like flames of fire, dispersed among them and resting on each one and they began to speak in their own tongues as the Spirit gave them utterance. Now there were living in Jerusalem devout Jews drawn from every nation under heaven all bewildered because each one heard his own language being spoken. "Why these men who are speaking are all Galileans, are they not? How is it then that we hear them, each of us in his own native language? Parthians, Medes, Elamites; inhabitants of Mesopotamia, of Judea and Cappadocia…we hear them telling in our own tongues the great things God has done." And they were perplexed, saying to one another, "What can this mean?" (Acts 2:1–11)

What a marvelous precedent for group spiritual direction! What indeed can this mean? It can only mean, I think, that wherever people are willing to gather together in silence, acknowledging the holy and waiting for the promptings of the Spirit, something very good can happen. Differences are transcended. In the common language of desire, people are able to hear—each in his or her own tongue—God's presence in the lives of one another. The spirit of Love is poured forth for them and for our world! It is enough!

Contributors

Editors

Rose Mary Dougherty, S.S.N.D., began the process of group spiritual direction at Shalem Institute in 1987 and has nurtured its organic growth. She has authored the book and video, *Group Spiritual Direction: Community for Discernment.*

Monica Maxon has edited Shalem's publications for more than twenty years, including the Shalem News and copyediting for the book *Living with Apocalypse.* She has a masters degree in theological studies.

Lynne Smith is a member of Shalem's board of directors and longtime participant, facilitator, and mentor for facilitators of group spiritual direction at Shalem since its beginning. She has been published in the *Shalem News.*

Contributors

Tom Adams, a Roman Catholic layman, has participated in group spiritual direction with Shalem for ten years. He works as a management and leadership transition consultant with non-profit organizations in the Baltimore-Washington area and with national foundations.

Franklin Adkinson is a physician and longtime participant in group spiritual direction. He is an increasingly committed ecumenist who has recently served as senior warden in his Episcopal parish, where he now chairs the committee on prayer and spiritual formation.

Margaret Benefiel is a Quaker who teaches at theological schools and does consulting and spiritual direction for organizations. She is widely published, most recently co-authoring a chapter in the book, *The Hidden Spirit: Discovering the Spirit of Institutions.*

Nancy Brousseau, O.P., is director of the Institute of Spirituality at Dominican Center at Marywood in Grand Rapids, Michigan. She supervises holistic ministry, prayer and ritual, spiritual formation programs, and spiritual direction and spiritual companioning programs, and also offers group spiritual direction for the general public and for the homeless.

Judith Brown Bryan is a certified social worker and full-time student at Colgate Rochester Divinity School, studying for ordained ministry. She and Trevor Watt have worked together in a church setting to provide group spiritual direction.

Ken Clansky is a Roman Catholic layman and eucharistic minister. He is a partner in a small electronic publishing business. He also has a certificate in theology from Georgetown University and has been a participant in group spiritual direction at Shalem for about ten years.

Trudy Dervan is a Roman Catholic laywoman and graduate of Shalem's Spiritual Guidance Program.

Tilden Edwards, an Episcopal priest, is the founder of the Shalem Institute and author of numerous books on spirituality, including *Spiritual Friend,* and *Spiritual Director, Spiritual Companion: Guide to Tending the Soul.*

Liz Ellmann, M.Div., serves as adjunct faculty in Seattle University's Executive Leadership Program, where she is experimenting with ways to incorporate group spiritual direction into organizational life. As a Roman Catholic lay minister, she founded SoulTenders to support people in the workplace who want to integrate their spiritual values and their work. She also is a spiritual director in the Puget Sound Spiritual Exercises in Everyday Life.

Rosemary Eyre-Brook, a pediatric anesthesiologist, has been involved with Shalem for nearly twelve years and is a longtime participant in group spiritual direction. She is currently working on a masters degree at Wesley Theological Seminary.

Gordon Forbes is a retired minister and poet. He recently published a book titled *Sower, Seed and Soil: Sermons and Poems from a Mainline Church.*

Contributors

Meg Greeley has initiated group spiritual direction in at least five rural parishes in Colorado. She is a spiritual director and coordinator of prayer ministries at an Episcopal church in Golden, Colorado.

Don Kelley is a member of the Independent Christian Community. He is a staff member for Still Point Ministries in Asheville, North Carolina, and works as a self-employed planning consultant for nonprofit organizations. He has facilitated both clergy and parish-based groups for spiritual direction.

James Kennedy, a Roman Catholic layman, has been in group spiritual direction at Shalem for four years and has attended several Shalem workshops. He is also involved with a Christian AIDS ministry for homeless men and mentors a teenaged boy in a county government program. He is an engineer and works for a federal agency on nuclear waste disposal.

Ann Kline is committed to exploring and developing contemplative prayer within the context of Judaism and has initiated group spiritual direction at a conservative synagogue. She works part-time as an attorney for the U.S. Environmental Protection Agency, is a hospice volunteer, and writes regularly for a hospice newsletter.

Lois Lindbloom has facilitated groups for spiritual direction in her at-home setting and is now mentoring others who are facilitating group spiritual direction. She is a pastoral care associate in her local Baptist church, is a graduate of Shalem's Spiritual Guidance Program, and is a licensed psychologist.

Anne Lipe is a lifelong Lutheran and has worked as both a music therapy clinician and educator. Currently, she is developing a retreat and spiritual direction ministry and hopes to do research on the interconnections among music, spirituality, and health. She has been a participant in group spiritual direction at Shalem for ten years.

Don MacDougall is a retired pastor in the United Church of Canada. He is director of the ecumenical Atlantic Jubilee Program in Spiritual Guidance, where he has initiated group spiritual direction.

Patricia McCulloch, M.H.S.H., has been a youth and parish minister in a large Roman Catholic church, where she has facilitated group spiritual direction with both youth and adults. She is the author of *Take Five* (Ave Maria Press).

Gigi Ross graduated from Washington Theological Union with a graduate certificate in spiritual direction, and she has a M.F.A. in creative writing from American University. She is a registrar at the Shalem Institute.

Susan Skillen is lay associate for spiritual direction at her Episcopal church. She has led a number of spiritual direction groups and leads retreats and discernment days for her parish and other churches in the Boston area, as well as leading retreats regularly in Italy.

Doug Tanner is a Methodist minister and executive director for the Faith & Politics Institute, a nonpartisan, interfaith organization whose mission is to provide occasions for moral reflection

and spiritual community for political leaders. He has participated in group spiritual direction and incorporates his experience into his work on Capitol Hill.

A. J. van den Blink, Ph.D., is an Episcopal priest who teaches
in the department of pastoral theology at Colgate Rochester
Divinity School, where he facilitates group spiritual direction
with divinity school students.

Trevor Watt is a United Church of Christ minister who works as
parish associate for spiritual formation in a Presbyterian church
where he has introduced group spiritual direction. He taught
interdisciplinary social science at SUNY Buffalo for thirty years
and is now professor of systematic theology and psychology at
Canisius College.